Foreclosing the Dream

Foreclosing
the Dream

*How America's Housing Crisis Is
Reshaping Our Cities and Suburbs*

William H. Lucy

American Planning Association
Planners Press

Making Great Communities Happen

Chicago | Washington, D.C.

Contents

Tables and Figures

TABLES

vii

FIGURES

Preface

When a strong trend is in its early stage, it does not look strong. Is that where city revival is now? I think so. The trend line is similar for several indicators—including income, housing value, race, and recently population—and in the direction of city revival for each one. When suburbanization was well under way after World War II, the 1950 census did not contain clear evidence proclaiming what would happen during the next half century. But an incipient trend became a wave, and the decline of cities coincided with the rise of suburbs.

Since then, suburban prosperity—and spatial sprawl on the edges of suburbs—has seemed to be the unvarying companion of city decline. Yet recently, that relationship has lost its certainty, dramatically so.

The answer to two questions contains the seeds of a revolution in perceptions and reality. The first question is: Which metropolitan area had the fastest central-city revival after 1990? The second question is: Which metropolitan area had the fastest suburban population sprawl, adding the most counties to its metropolitan area since 2000?

The answer to each question is Atlanta. Thus, rapid suburban sprawl does not inevitably cause central-city decline. Sprawl may even nurture rapid city revival in some instances—an unthinkable thought until now.

Which conditions have brought about this change in metropolitan areas? How widespread are these changing conditions? Have they been perpetuated by foreclosures during the financial crisis of 2008 and 2009? Perhaps locations of foreclosures are the final piece of evidence signaling transformation of post–World War II patterns of the well-off living in suburbs and the poor living in cities.

This year, 2010, has 65 years of suburban sprawl to live with or unravel. Higher gasoline prices indicate traveling shorter distances each day is wise, so unraveling sprawl is the better option. Signs of global warming tell us that time is short for altering our way of life. These conditions make compact redevelopment necessary. As the suburban dream is foreclosed, the time for a different dream has arrived.

Acknowledgments

I do not have a long list of people to thank for assistance, just four special ones.

David Phillips, Professor of Urban and Environmental Planning at the University of Virginia, has worked with me for 30 years as collaborative conceptualizer, insightful editor, indicator strategist, data manager, and cowriter. This book reflects our work over the years, especially our book *Tomorrow's Cities, Tomorrow's Suburbs* (APA Planners Press, 2006), which emphasized changes in trends during the 1990s. In addition, a coauthored paper included some of the preliminary findings through 2006 on trends in cities and metropolitan areas.

Jeff Herlitz, my graduate research assistant at the University of Virginia, produced the maps of metropolitan foreclosure patterns, the national map of foreclosures, and the detailed tables of 50 state and 236 county foreclosure patterns in 2008. These foreclosure data patterns provided the basis for the foreclosure analysis that supplemented income and housing-value trend data, enhancing my confidence that strong trends toward revival of cities have emerged since 2000 from a slow beginning during the 1980s and 1990s.

Timothy Mennel, senior editor at APA Planners Press, navigated the publisher's decision to publish a facsimile of the manuscript I submitted. He also proposed that we engage a writer to increase accessibility of the published work.

I suggested asking David Peterson, reporter and writer with the Minneapolis *StarTribune* to contribute. After reading most of the manuscript, David said he was enthusiastic about working on it and modestly suggested the material could use some "narrative propulsion." We returned to that goal periodically to evaluate progress, which included many examples to illustrate themes. I have profited from our collaboration.

Tim Mennel occasionally congratulated us on our progress, but he noted tersely that we weren't there yet. He was right. Are we there yet? I hope so. The work is vastly better than my submission draft.

1

The Ring of Death

In the fall of 2008, a suburban police detective named Chris Olson took a close look for the first time at an America just minutes from where he worked.

Olson worked in Prior Lake, half an hour south of Minneapolis. Prior Lake is located along the outermost ring of suburbia: once you leave it, it's farm fields. And beyond the farm fields are exurban outposts and small rural towns, sleepy until recently but suddenly now sprouting outcroppings of beige townhomes and suburban-style subdivisions. Prior Lake itself is full of expensive lakeshore property, but these outposts, such as the twin merged communities of Elko and New Market, best known as the home of bars and raucous stock-car races, are much more blue-collar places. They are places to which, as developers like to say, people of modest means "drive 'til they reach 'Affordability,'" trading long commutes and inconvenience for a price-to-house-size ratio they could never find closer in.

In the fall of 2008, Olson ran for county commissioner for a district that included much of the more outlying area of the county. He door-knocked his district: walked it from house to house to house. And he emerged from the experience aghast.

"There's an alarming number of empty houses," he said.

I'm flabbergasted. It's staggering. Nothing good can come from this. It's just a matter of time, without maintenance, that these structures will degrade to the point where they are worthless. They've been vacant for months. The grass is knee high. There are probably 50 to 100 of them in Elko–New Market alone.

It is abundantly clear that this has to be addressed quickly. It's a public safety concern and a huge economic concern: the city is lacking revenue. And it's not just low-income areas; there are a lot of middle-income areas riddled with empty homes. Foreclosure notices in the windows; "no trespassing" signs; noxious weeds. Someone from the city should be mowing these lawns.

Whether or not city officials in Elko–New Market were paying attention to what was going on along their twisting subdivision streets and cul-de-sacs, their counterparts in other communities on the metropolitan fringe were learning to do so. Homes that had once been nothing but good news to a community—sources of growth, of swelling tax rolls—were now suddenly turning into liabilities, even in newly developing, upscale communities, as foreclosed and abandoned homes fell apart from neglect.

An almost $700,000 Andover house that sat empty for months with a flooded basement, growing mold, recently sold at an auction for $280,000. On a quiet cul-de-sac in Champlin, inspectors were finally able to get into an empty house last week that was soaked with more than 200,000 gallons of water from a burst pipe. Ceilings had collapsed in the basement, the wood floors had warped and mold was growing along the baseboards.[1]

Entrepreneurs in the private sector had also perked up—and were seeing opportunities. They were sending teams of workers out to these homes to do cleanups. In Farmington, a newly developing middle-income suburb a few minutes' drive to the east of Elko–New Market that had just got done building a $96 million showpiece high school with half a million dollars' worth of artificial turf, "trash-out" workers went from home to home, collecting the belongings of owners forced out of their homes.

Ryan Gorman, 22, of Cottage Grove, finds a blanket in one of the bedrooms and spreads it near the doorway as a makeshift garbage sack. Next, he picks up a shovel and starts scooping debris onto the blanket—everything from clothing and a Christmas wreath to paper that's been shredded by mice.

Across the hall, Carol Perkins, 41, of St. Paul, uses a shovel to trash out what's left of a child's room. At least 30 empty containers of milk, juice or yogurt are under the bed. Amid a sea of debris that extends nearly wall to wall are some familiar chums of childhood—Elmo and Big Bird, Tigger and Nemo.

It all winds up out front in a Dumpster, where the metal thunders as Whiting smashes a bedroom unit into a pile of boards.[2]

All across the country, the same kinds of things were happening. In Atlanta, a journalist spoke of a new species of "zombie subdivision"—places with "few if any completed homes and a weedy patch where the swim-and-tennis center was planned."[3] They were sitting all across the sprawling Atlanta metro, it seemed, but were most prevalent in the outermost rings.

The main problem is sheer volume—a staggering 150,000 vacant housing lots across metro Atlanta are available, more than a decade's supply at current absorption rates. The median sale price for empty lots has plunged from $57,000 at the height of the housing boom in 2007 to $30,000 this year, according to Smart Numbers, a Marietta company that tracks the local real estate market. . . .

Sitting in front of a computer at his home office, [Smart Numbers's Steve] Palm pulls up a color-coded map of metro Atlanta showing lot supply by U.S. Census tract. An ominous arc of dark reds and browns encircles Atlanta.

"This is the ring of death," he said.

In places like that, home owners had two choices: either property values dropped because theirs was one of just a few homes in a 21st-century ghost town, or they dropped because a developer was buying up empty land at half the previous price and selling the completed homes at a correspondingly low rate. "It's better to have some neighbors and have the development built out than have it look deserted," a researcher was quoted as saying. "Unless you prefer there being only five houses in a 300-lot development, so you can go and hit some golf balls."

In other, more completed neighborhoods, a severe drop in value was changing the socioeconomics of home buyers. A journalist tracking life in a Los Angeles suburb found:

> A carpet cleaner who had moved from a small apartment near Los Angeles was brought to tears the first time he cleaned the rugs in his new four-bedroom home. A maintenance worker at a bakery who had waited two years for the bank to accept his offer on a foreclosed home now spends weekends proudly building an addition. A multigenerational family arrived in Beth Court from a mobile home. . . .
>
> Ted Hanson, 71, who lives with his wife, Connie, at the entrance to Beth Court, on adjoining Parkland Avenue, views the changes in the neighborhood through three basic prisms: falling home values, growing safety concerns and blighted lawns.[4]

What united all these developments, all these extraordinary new kinds of images, was that they were not how things had traditionally worked in America.

Whether or not Americans consciously thought of it this way, they had grown accustomed over many decades to thinking of two basic paradigms when it came to cities and neighborhoods. One strand in this narrative was the flight from the aging, battered, decaying industrial Northeast and Midwest toward the new, sunny, glittering Sun Belt—and toward the not quite so sunny but hip, artsy, literate, bike-path-laced, latte-sipping cities such as Seattle, Portland, Denver, and Minneapolis. The other strand was the flight away from aging, battered, decaying, crime-plagued inner cities and out into the safe, leafy, pristine suburban fringe.

Yet what has been happening in those places recently was not really part of that game plan. The Sun Belt has been suffering. And everywhere the suburban fringe is suffering. The nation's bright new places—north, south, east, or west—seem to be precisely where all the problems are being played out. That was the source of Detective Olson's amazement: he didn't expect to see decay in a place that was brand-new.

This book aims to sort out precisely what is going on, and why, and what it means for the future—notably for the home buyers who worry about the long-term prospects for their massive investment of income and for the city officials whose job it is to anticipate the next stage of metropolitan development. In a city like Elko–New Market, after all, even a single squad car (an item that costs as much as many people pay for a home) is something saved for for years beforehand, in the expectation of continued growth. But what are the chances, these days, that that growth will actually materialize? Is the foreclosure pattern telling us something important?

The argument of this book is that the pattern of foreclosures is yet one more layer of evidence pointing us to a profound and rather sudden shift in the momentum of metropolitan development: a revival of cities and a drawing back from the exurban fervor that drove so much development and so much commentary in the closing decades of the last century. This shift has to do, among other things, with changing tastes in homes and neighborhoods; with changes in the demographic structures of American society; with changes in the cost and predictability of energy; and with a new consciousness of the cost to the earth of failing to restrain our volume of climate-changing emissions. All these shifts have come about within a period of time that will seem in retrospect to have been just a moment in historic time, and a moment that caught a lot of folks totally unprepared.

PATTERNS OF FORECLOSURE

Concentrations

Foreclosures have not been evenly distributed across the country. On the contrary, they have been happening in some places far, far more than in others.

The national foreclosure rate in 2008 was 0.79 percent of all housing units. Only seven states exceeded that rate. An eighth, Idaho, tied it. But the seven states exceeding it had considerably higher rates. Nevada's was five times higher: 4.10 percent. California's was 2.57 percent, Arizona's 2.26 percent, and Florida's 1.99 percent (Table 1.1). Seven of the top 10 foreclosure states were in the West. The other three were Florida, Illinois, and Connecticut.

TABLE 1.1 FORECLOSURE RATES, POPULATION GROWTH, AND MEDIAN OWNER-OCCUPIED HOUSING VALUE TO MEDIAN FAMILY INCOME RATIOS

State	FORE-CLOSURE RATE (RANK) 2008	POPULATION GROWTH (RANK) 1990–2000	POPULATION GROWTH (RANK) 2000–2007	MEDIAN HOUSING VALUE TO MEDIAN FAMILY INCOME RATIO (RANK) 2007
Nevada	4.10 (1)	66.3 (1)	27.1 (1)	5.13 (3)
California	2.57 (2)	13.8 (18)	7.5 (18)	8.30 (1)
Arizona	2.26 (3)	40.0 (2)	22.7 (2)	4.25 (9)
Florida	1.99 (4)	23.5 (7)	13.7 (7)	4.24 (10)
Illinois	1.61 (5)	8.6 (34)	3.3 (34)	3.17 (21t)
Colorado	1.38 (6)	30.6 (3)	12.3 (8)	3.60 (16)
Utah	1.03 (7)	29.6 (4)	17.9 (3)	3.24 (20)
Idaho	0.79 (8)	28.5 (5)	15.4 (5)	3.17 (21t)
Oregon	0.68 (9)	20.4 (11)	9.2 (13)	4.23 (11)
Connecticut	0.65 (10)	3.6 (47)	2.6 (38)	3.82 (14)
U.S. Avg.	0.79	—	—	3.16

Sources: foreclosure.com, U.S. Bureau of the Census, American Community Survey 2007, and Metropolitan Policy Center of the Brookings Institution 2008.

Even as news accounts were depicting the foreclosure crisis as a national issue having to do with abusive lending practices, skyrocketing prices, and other problems, foreclosure rates in most states were low. In three-fourths of the states, 38 to be precise, foreclosure rates were below 0.50 percent, or one in 200. In precisely one-half of the states, foreclosure rates were less than 0.25 percent, or one in 400. And in 11 states, foreclosure rates were below 0.10 percent, or one in 1,000 (Table 1.2).

Foreclosure processes in just four of the 50 states—California, Florida, Nevada, and Arizona—constituted 62 percent of the

U.S. total in 2008. And, as startling as that might sound, the pattern is even more highly specific than that.

Within three of those four states, foreclosures were concentrated in a few metropolitan areas. Clark County, meaning the entire Las Vegas metropolitan area, had 88 percent of Nevada's foreclosures. The two counties of Maricopa and Pinal, which together make up the entire Phoenix metro area, accounted for 91 percent of Arizona's foreclosures. In Florida, the metropolitan areas of Miami, Orlando, and Tampa–St. Petersburg contained 62 percent of all foreclosures. In California, foreclosures were more widely dispersed: the metropolitan areas of Los Angeles, Sacramento, San Diego, and San Francisco contained 63 percent of all foreclosures.

The concentration of foreclosures becomes even more vivid when brought down to individual counties. Forty percent of all 2008 foreclosures (402,213) were in 16 counties in 10 metropolitan areas. Twenty-nine percent (295,060) were in just eight counties (Los Angeles, Riverside, San Bernardino, San Diego, Maricopa, Clark, Broward, and Cook) in six metropolitan areas (Los Angeles, San Diego, Phoenix, Las Vegas, Miami, and Chicago) (see county data in Appendix 2).

Within the 35 most populous metropolitan areas, foreclosures were also concentrated. Recall that the national average in 2008 for housing units in foreclosure proceedings was 0.79 percent. In these 35 metropolitan areas, out of 236 with data, 74 counties had foreclosure rates at or above the national average. Thirty-three of these counties were in nine metropolitan areas, in California, Florida, Nevada, and Arizona, and foreclosure rates exceeded the national average in 30 of them (91 percent).[5]

Even more revealing is the discrepancy in the rate of foreclosures. Only 11 counties had foreclosure rates of 3 percent or more of total housing units (including units with and without mortgages) in 2008. They were: Clark (Las Vegas), 5.1 percent; Riverside and San Bernardino (Los Angeles), 4.5 and 4.0; Osceola (Orlando), 4.1; Broward (Miami), 3.9; Pinal and Maricopa (Phoenix), 3.2 and 3.3; Solano and Contra Costa (San Francisco), 3.7 and 3.4; Sacramento, 3.5; and Adams (Denver), 3.0.

TABLE 1.2 STATES' FORECLOSURES IN 2008 BY PERCENT OF HOUSING UNITS UNDER FORECLOSURE

STATE	FORECLOSURE DATA DATE	2008 FORECLOSURES AND PREFORECLOSURES	2007 HOUSING UNITS	NUMBER OF HOUSING UNITS TO FORECLOSURES AND PREFORCLOSURES	COMPARED TO U.S. TOTAL	% OF HOUSING UNITS UNDER FORECLOSURE OR PREFORECLOSURE
United States	10/16/2008	1,009,485	127,895,430	127		0.79
Alabama	10/20/2008	3,495	2,137,012	611	484.8	0.16
Alaska	10/20/2008	839	282,271	336	209.7	0.30
Arizona	10/16/2008	60,292	2,667,550	44	-82.4	2.26
Arkansas	10/20/2008	5,342	1,287,472	241	114.3	0.41
California	10/16/2008	342,445	13,308,705	39	-87.8	2.57
Colorado	10/16/2008	29,299	2,127,358	73	-54.1	1.38
Connecticut	10/20/2008	9,414	1,438,548	153	26.1	0.65
D.C.	10/20/2008	336	284,235	846	719.2	0.12
Delaware	10/20/2008	215	388,619	1,808	1,680.8	0.06
Florida	10/16/2008	173,231	8,716,601	50	-76.4	1.99
Georgia	10/20/2008	22,837	3,961,643	173	46.8	0.58
Hawaii	10/20/2008	349	506,751	1,452	1,325.3	0.07
Idaho	10/20/2008	4,999	631,022	126	-0.5	0.79
Illinois	10/16/2008	84,523	5,246,116	62	-64.6	1.61
Indiana	10/20/2008	6,587	2,777,953	422	295.0	0.24
Iowa	10/16/2008	1,186	1,329,388	1,121	994.2	0.09
Kansas	10/16/2008	985	1,219,100	1,238	1,111.0	0.08
Kentucky	10/20/2008	3,713	1,906,198	513	386.7	0.19
Louisiana	10/20/2008	1,006	1,858,586	1,848	1,720.8	0.05
Maine	10/20/2008	397	696,681	1,755	1,628.2	0.06
Maryland	10/20/2008	3,312	2,318,430	700	573.3	0.14
Massachusetts	10/20/2008	7,861	2,722,323	346	219.6	0.29
Michigan	10/20/2008	17,839	4,526,914	254	127.1	0.39
Minnesota	10/20/2008	8,834	2,304,473	261	134.2	0.38

2007 MEDIAN VALUE OF OWNER-OCCUPIED HOUSING	2007 MEDIAN FAMILY INCOME	RATIO OF HOUSING VALUE TO MEDIAN FAMILY INCOME	2000 MEDIAN VALUE OF OWNER-OCCUPIED HOUSING	2000 MEDIAN FAMILY INCOME	RATIO OF HOUSING VALUE TO MEDIAN FAMILY INCOME	% CHANGE IN RATIO FROM 2000 TO 2007
$194,300	$61,173	3.2	$119,600	$50,046	2.4	33.30
$115,600	$50,770	2.3	$85,100	$41,657	2.0	15.00
$231,300	$72,865	3.2	$144,200	$59,036	2.4	33.30
$237,700	$58,627	4.1	$121,300	$46,723	2.6	57.60
$101,000	$47,021	2.1	$72,800	$38,663	1.9	10.50
$532,300	$67,484	7.9	$211,500	$53,025	4.0	97.50
$233,900	$67,491	3.5	$166,600	$55,883	3.0	16.60
$309,200	$81,421	3.8	$166,900	$65,521	2.5	52.00
$450,900	$66,672	6.8	$157,200	$46,283	3.4	100.00
$239,700	$66,198	3.6	$130,400	$55,257	2.4	50.00
$230,400	$56,966	4.0	$105,500	$45,625	2.3	73.90
$164,500	$58,403	2.8	$111,200	$49,280	2.3	21.70
$555,400	$73,879	7.5	$272,200	$56,961	4.8	56.20
$178,100	$54,342	3.3	$106,300	$43,490	2.4	37.50
$208,800	$65,761	3.2	$130,800	$55,545	2.4	33.30
$122,900	$57,734	2.1	$94,300	$50,261	1.9	10.50
$117,900	$59,587	2.0	$82,500	$48,005	1.7	17.60
$121,200	$60,510	2.0	$83,500	$49,624	1.7	17.60
$114,300	$50,291	2.3	$86,700	$40,939	2.1	9.50
$126,800	$50,727	2.5	$85,000	$39,774	2.1	19.00
$176,000	$56,266	3.1	$98,700	$45,179	2.2	40.90
$347,000	$82,404	4.2	$146,000	$61,876	2.4	75.00
$366,400	$78,497	4.7	$185,700	$61,664	3.0	56.60
$153,100	$59,618	2.6	$115,600	$53,457	2.2	18.10
$213,600	$69,172	3.1	$122,400	$56,874	2.2	40.90

TABLE 1.2 (CONTINUED)

STATE	FORECLOSURE DATA DATE	2008 FORECLOSURES AND PREFORECLOSURES	2007 HOUSING UNITS	NUMBER OF HOUSING UNITS TO FORECLOSURES AND PREFORCLOSURES	COMPARED TO U.S. TOTAL	% OF HOUSING UNITS UNDER FORECLOSURE OR PREFORECLOSURE
Mississippi	10/20/2008	1,850	1,254,936	678	551.7	0.15
Missouri	10/20/2008	12,762	2,647,379	207	80.7	0.48
Montana	10/20/2008	842	435,586	517	390.6	0.19
Nebraska	10/20/2008	2,345	780,592	333	206.2	0.30
Nevada	10/16/2008	45,147	1,102,409	24	-102.3	4.10
New Hampshire	10/20/2008	1,007	594,126	590	463.3	0.17
New Jersey	10/16/2008	15,786	3,498,786	222	94.9	0.45
New Mexico	10/20/2008	2,750	862,095	313	186.8	0.32
New York	10/16/2008	13,198	7,940,072	602	474.9	0.17
North Carolina	10/20/2008	5,432	4,124,066	759	632.5	0.13
North Dakota	10/20/2008	42	310,438	7,391	7,264.7	0.01
Ohio	10/16/2008	14,848	5,065,254	341	214.4	0.29
Oklahoma	10/16/2008	5,678	1,623,100	286	159.2	0.35
Oregon	10/20/2008	10,944	1,609,764	147	20.4	0.68
Pennsylvania	10/16/2008	10,320	5,478,158	531	404.1	0.19
Rhode Island	10/20/2008	1,147	450,877	393	266.4	0.25
South Carolina	10/20/2008	2,873	2,022,033	704	577.1	0.14
South Dakota	10/20/2008	115	356,264	3,098	2,971.3	0.03
Tennessee	10/20/2008	5,978	2,724,929	456	329.1	0.22
Texas	10/16/2008	36,151	9,433,119	261	134.2	0.38
Utah	10/20/2008	9,563	925,295	97	-29.9	1.03
Vermont	10/20/2008	101	311,420	3,083	2,956.7	0.03

2007 MEDIAN VALUE OF OWNER-OCCUPIED HOUSING	2007 MEDIAN FAMILY INCOME	RATIO OF HOUSING VALUE TO MEDIAN FAMILY INCOME	2000 MEDIAN VALUE OF OWNER-OCCUPIED HOUSING	2000 MEDIAN FAMILY INCOME	RATIO OF HOUSING VALUE TO MEDIAN FAMILY INCOME	% CHANGE IN RATIO FROM 2000 TO 2007
$96,000	$44,769	2.1	$71,400	$37,406	1.9	10.50
$138,600	$55,947	2.5	$89,900	$46,044	2.0	25.00
$170,000	$53,497	3.2	$99,500	$40,487	2.5	28.00
$122,200	$58,587	2.1	$88,000	$48,032	1.8	16.60
$311,300	$62,842	5.0	$142,000	$50,849	2.8	78.50
$261,800	$74,625	3.5	$133,300	$57,575	2.3	52.10
$372,300	$81,823	4.6	$170,800	$65,370	2.6	76.90
$155,400	$49,658	3.1	$108,100	$39,425	2.7	14.80
$311,000	$64,602	4.8	$148,700	$51,691	2.9	65.50
$145,700	$55,028	2.6	$108,300	$46,335	2.3	13.00
$106,800	$58,827	1.8	$74,400	$43,654	1.7	5.80
$137,800	$58,374	2.4	$103,700	$50,037	2.1	14.20
$103,000	$51,787	2.0	$70,700	$40,709	1.7	17.60
$257,300	$59,152	4.3	$152,100	$48,680	3.1	38.70
$155,000	$60,825	2.5	$97,000	$49,184	2.0	25.00
$292,800	$70,187	4.2	$133,000	$52,781	2.5	68.00
$133,900	$52,913	2.5	$94,900	$44,227	2.1	19.00
$118,700	$53,910	2.2	$79,600	$43,237	1.8	22.20
$130,800	$51,945	2.5	$93,000	$43,517	2.1	19.00
$120,900	$55,742	2.2	$82,500	$45,861	1.8	22.20
$218,700	$62,432	3.5	$146,100	$51,022	2.9	20.60
$205,400	$61,561	3.3	$111,500	$48,625	2.3	43.40

TABLE 1.2 (CONTINUED)

STATE	FORECLOSURE DATA DATE	2008 FORECLOSURES AND PREFORECLOSURES	2007 HOUSING UNITS	NUMBER OF HOUSING UNITS TO FORECLOSURES AND PREFORCLOSURES	COMPARED TO U.S. TOTAL	% OF HOUSING UNITS UNDER FORECLOSURE OR PREFORECLOSURE
Virginia	10/16/2008	7,380	3,273,206	444	316.8	0.23
Washington	10/20/2008	15,064	2,744,324	182	55.5	0.55
West Virginia	10/20/2008	601	882,631	1,469	1,341.9	0.07
Wisconsin	10/16/2008	9,499	2,558,278	269	142.6	0.37
Wyoming	10/20/2008	86	242,344	2,818	2,691.3	0.04

2008 Foreclosures and Preforeclosures are from www.foreclosure.com.
2007 Housing Units are from the American Community Survey in November 2008.
2007 Median Value of Owner-Occupied Housing and Median Family Income are from the American Community Survey in November .

In some ways the most important pattern of all to note is the location of the hardest-hit counties. Many early news reports emphasized the inner city concentration of foreclosures. And some visual depictions of the problem tended to reinforce this impression. In Omaha, for instance, in the summer of 2009, the *World-Herald* published a map that made it look as though the problem was most severe in neighborhoods close to the urban core and tended to grow less pronounced the further out you went.[6] But this map included only two of the eight counties in the Omaha–Council Bluffs metropolitan area.

In order to sort out what was really going on, it is vital to see the spatial patterns in these foreclosures: not just the relatively limited number of counties with the most serious problem, but where they are located on each metropolitan area's map.

Cities versus Suburbs

It can be harder to gauge exactly where foreclosures are happening than to pin down other kinds of facts about housing. That's because foreclosures tend to be counted up by county.

2007 MEDIAN VALUE OF OWNER-OCCUPIED HOUSING	2007 MEDIAN FAMILY INCOME	RATIO OF HOUSING VALUE TO MEDIAN FAMILY INCOME	2000 MEDIAN VALUE OF OWNER-OCCUPIED HOUSING	2000 MEDIAN FAMILY INCOME	RATIO OF HOUSING VALUE TO MEDIAN FAMILY INCOME	% CHANGE IN RATIO FROM 2000 TO 2007
$262,100	$70,894	3.7	$125,400	$54,169	2.3	60.80
$300,800	$66,642	4.5	$168,300	$53,760	3.1	45.10
$96,000	$46,338	2.1	$72,800	$36,484	2.0	5.00
$168,800	$62,804	2.7	$112,200	$52,911	2.1	28.50
$172,300	$63,947	2.7	$96,600	$45,685	2.1	28.50

And many counties across the country are grab bags of differing circumstances, containing everything from urban high-rise towers at their centers to 600-acre farms at their edges.

In eight big metropolitan areas, however, one can fillet out the central cities from their suburbs, because central cities are also counties. In other metropolitan areas, data for central cities are hidden from view in foreclosure data for the counties of which the central cities constitute an undetermined percentage of the county totals. Not all of these eight areas behaved in the same ways. But, broadly speaking, the central city usually had a lower foreclosure rate than at least one of its surrounding suburban counties—and sometimes several.

In the San Francisco metropolitan area, suburban Solano County had 3.69 percent of its housing units in foreclosure in November 2008 (Figure 1.1). The comparable figure for the city of San Francisco: just 0.24 percent—a ratio of 15 to 1. Each of the eight counties in the San Francisco metropolitan area had a higher foreclosure rate than the central city. Six counties exceeded the national foreclosure rate.

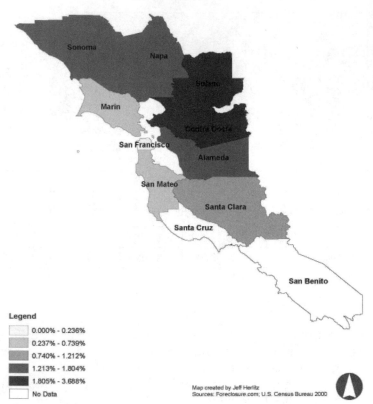

Figure 1.1   San Francisco
Percent of Units under Foreclosure or Preforeclosure (2008)

The Washington, D.C., area had the second-greatest dispar-
ity between a foreclosure rate for a central city (0.12) and that
of its highest suburban county (1.27 percent, in Prince William
County, a 1 to 10 ratio). Twelve of 13 cities and counties had
higher foreclosure rates than the District of Columbia. In Prince
William County, foreclosures skyrocketed from 52 in 2005, to
282 in 2006, to 3,344 in 2007.[7]

In New York City, of five metro counties, the lowest foreclosure rate (0.04) was in Manhattan. In Staten Island (part of the
city, but an outlying, more residential part and a county unto
itself, called Richmond) the rate was 0.77. The metropolitan

high point was 1.52, in Passaic County, across the river in New Jersey (see Appendix 1).

Elsewhere, three other central cities had foreclosure rates that were low but not much different from the highest rate in other counties:

Philadelphia: 0.53 percent; 0.59 percent in Camden County
Norfolk: 0.19 percent; 0.24 percent in Suffolk County
Baltimore: 0.16 percent; 0.10 in the next lowest county

In each of these central cities, the foreclosure rate was well below the national rate of 0.79 percent.

In Denver, the central city foreclosure rate (2.23 percent) was higher than the national rate. But it was higher still in Adams County (3.01 percent). In St. Louis, the rate was 1.02 percent, but that was lower than that of two counties in Illinois: St. Clair (1.71 percent) and Madison (1.21 percent).

There was no evidence, in other words, that foreclosures were concentrated in central cities. On the contrary, there were signs that foreclosures were concentrated elsewhere, sometimes in counties far from their central cities.

In other metros, the patterns are more complex because central cities are part of mixed counties. Data for the city of Chicago are included with other Cook County communities, but Chicago does contribute most of the residents and housing units. Cook County had a rather high foreclosure rate: 2.00 percent of housing units (Figure 1.3). Three outer counties (Kane, Kendall, and Will) had higher rates (2.24, 2.62, and 2.29 percent).

The Minneapolis–St. Paul area contains a particularly tricky county, Hennepin, which includes Minneapolis and contains everything from inner city trouble spots to 30-acre lakeside estates located half an hour's drive away. That said, Hennepin's rate (0.33 percent) was moderate (Figure 1.4). The more consistently urban Ramsey County (St. Paul and its older, closer-in suburbs) stood at 0.83 percent. The average for all 10 metro counties was 0.69 percent. The highest foreclosure rates were in Dakota, a suburban county with middle-aged inner-ring suburbs to its north and brand-new subdivisions sprinkled

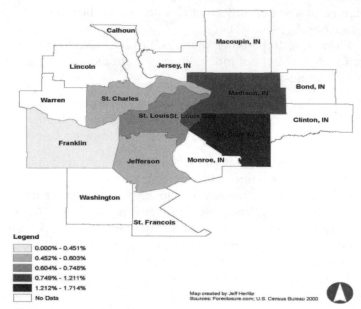

Figure 1.2   St. Louis
Percent of Units under Foreclosure or Preforeclosure (2008)

amid farms to its south (1.15 percent), and the almost exclusively exurban Wright County (1.48 percent), which for many years has been one of the state's fastest growing fringe areas. (See Appendix 1.)

In 2009, housing officials in Minnesota produced a map of the highest concentrations of foreclosures and vacant homes, broken down in a more fine-grained way than just by county (Figure 1.5). This map drills down to the level of census tracts.

Broadly speaking, the lesson of this map is that the problem is bad, to be sure, in some of the poorest of inner city areas and a handful of inner-ring suburbs; but then it skips over the more prosperous and longer-established suburbs (save for a few exceptions, often newly developing townhome areas within long-established cities) to take up residence in the exurbs. The darker swaths in the upper left-hand quadrant, across the very top, and across the very bottom are the areas of new semirural growth, including the city of Elko–New Market, at

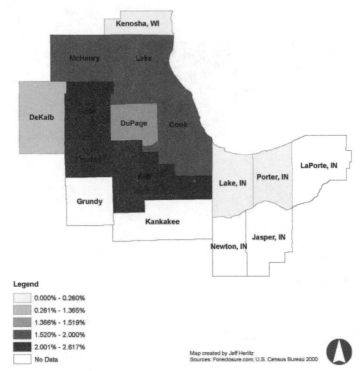

Figure 1.3 Chicago
Percent of Units under Foreclosure or Preforeclosure (2008)

center bottom. These are counties that for many years ranked among the top 100 fastest growing in the nation, including Scott County, lower left, on whose board Detective Olson was seeking a seat. Owing to a newly widened bridge cutting the commute to major job concentrations to its north, Scott County briefly ranked among the 10 fastest growing counties—out of more than 3,000—in the entire nation.

In October 2009, nearly one year after the 2008 foreclosure patterns described above, the central cities and central counties still had lower foreclosure rates than outer counties in their metropolitan areas (the cities of San Francisco, St. Louis, and Washington, D.C., and the counties of Hennepin and Ramsey around Minneapolis and St. Paul).

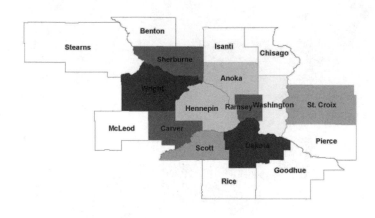

Figure 1.4   Minneapolis
Percent of Units under Foreclosure or Preforeclosure (2008)

What is to be made of this pattern? If suburbs and exurbs, if the bright new places, are being hit as hard or harder than cities, is it just that so many of the mortgages there are newer? One way to double-check is to look at parallel indicators, such as the value of homes.

THE PATTERN OF HOME VALUES

In the spring of 2009, newspaper readers in Southern California awoke to a startling piece of news. Thousands of homes within commuting range of Los Angeles were now worth less than they had been in 1989, 20 years earlier. Even "houses barely 20 years old and in decent shape [had] lost every dime of their appreciation, giving back not just the gains of the recent bubble but steady increases logged over a generation."[8] A UCLA economist described this as something that had never happened before.

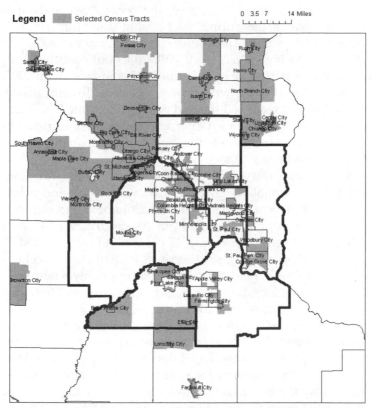

Legend Selected Census Tracts

0 3.5 7   14 Miles

Census tracts with an index score of 18 or higher on either the foreclosure or vacancy scale

Minnesota Housing

Figure 1.5   Minnesota Census Tracts Qualifying for NSP-2 Funds

There was a pattern to these losses. Most of the homes with severe declines in value were located at the metropolitan fringe, long drives away from the center, in cities like Palmdale, a rapidly growing community an hour or more away from the center of Los Angeles.

The value of homes is a more precise indicator than foreclosures, because there is easy access to evidence of what's happening at the level of cities and even neighborhoods.

In the Washington, D.C., area, the central city and inner suburbs were stable during the housing downturn of 2007, while two large middle and outer suburbs in northern Virginia have lost housing value. Prince William County was hit hardest, losing 16 percent of its value in 2007 compared with 2006, while Loudoun County went down 10 percent. To compensate, Prince William increased the real property tax rate 27 percent and Loudoun increased it 19 percent. In contrast, Fairfax and Arlington counties, closer to the center, and the City of Alexandria increased taxes 3.3 to 3.6 percent.[9]

A comparison of single-unit house sales in the Washington, D.C., metropolitan area for 2007 and 2008 found prices increased 8 percent in the District of Columbia and declined in other jurisdictions—5 percent in Alexandria, 7 percent in Arlington, 14 percent in Fairfax, 17 percent in Loudoun, and 23 percent in Prince William.[10] In Prince William, price declines in its six zip codes ranged from 49 percent to only 6 percent.[11] Prices rose in the center of the metropolitan area and fell more with greater distance from the center.

Of course, foreclosures can themselves influence an area's average home value. But even when foreclosures are removed from the equation, home values follow a similar path. In the Minneapolis–St. Paul metro in the summer of 2009, a consultant—retained by the real estate industry in an effort to prove that home values were sustaining themselves better than foreclosure-stained numbers were suggesting—produced a table omitting all lender-mediated transactions. Table 1.3 shows the parts of town—"MLS Areas," meaning multiple-listing service areas, a real estate industry designation—with the biggest declines in value from 2006 to 2009.

The six worst-hit areas are mostly high-poverty city neighborhoods, typically close to downtown. Brooklyn Center is an inner-ring suburb adjacent to the traditional center for African Americans in the area; it is now the first Twin Cities suburb ever to have a majority of racial and ethnic minorities. But beyond those six, the problem starts to jump to the outskirts of town. Big Lake Township is an exurb, and so are a number of areas as you move up this list: northern Anoka County; Rice

TABLE 1.3 2006 MEDIAN HOME SALES PRICES COMPARED TO SECOND QUARTER 2009 TRADITIONAL HOME MEDIAN SALES PRICES, BY MLS AREA

CODE	MLS AREA	2006 ($)	SECOND QUARTER 2009 ($)	PERCENT CHANGE 2006–2009
769	Anoka	200,873	169,000	(15.9)
650	Belle Plaine	214,125	179,900	(16.0)
711	Southern Chisago County	211,900	174,900	(17.5)
648	New Prague/ New Market–Elko	250,000	204,876	(18.0)
398	Victoria	477,500	390,000	(18.3)
364	Brooklyn Park	230,825	186,250	(19.3)
707	Ham Lake	340,000	274,000	(19.4)
768	Fridley	209,900	168,405	(19.8)
713	Bethel	240,500	192,900	(19.8)
632	Rice County	187,650	150,000	(20.1)
758	Northwestern Anoka County	232,000	184,500	(20.5)
710	Northeastern Anoka County	279,950	221,000	(21.1)
714	St. Paul–Phalen	176,450	135,000	(23.5)
754	Big Lake Township	211,000	157,500	(25.4)
716	St. Paul–Hillcrest/ Hazel Park/ Dayton's Bluff	176,000	131,000	(25.6)
307	Minneapolis–Phillips	191,580	140,000	(26.9)
363	Brooklyn Center	192,925	137,900	(28.5)
301	Minneapolis–Camden	164,000	112,000	(31.7)
742	St. Paul–Central	153,000	99,900	(34.7)
305	Minneapolis–North	153,000	98,500	(35.6)

Source: Minneapolis Area Association of Realtors

County, which borders Elko–New Market; and so on.[12] Most are areas of modest incomes, as the values of homes suggest; but not all are modest: Victoria (as column three of Table 1.3 hints) is a very nice spot indeed, though by local standards a long drive from jobs: 40 minutes from downtown at top cruising speed in the middle of the night.

What about the places holding their value, or even increasing it, despite all the turmoil in the housing market? Other than Detective Olson's home turf of Prior Lake, which owes its success to its being made up almost entirely of lakeshore, the one thing all these places have in common is that they are located very close to major job centers. (See Table 1.4.) Two of them, codes 302 and 741, are right downtown—places that "back in the day," meaning in this case five or 10 years ago, would have consisted, residentially speaking, of little more than jails, flophouses, homeless shelters, and drug treatment centers.

In other words, the conventional American pattern of a flight outward from old and noisy and decaying toward new and serene and leafy-green, with values declining in the center and rising at the fringe, was seeing some intriguing new twists.

WHAT ACCOUNTS FOR THESE PATTERNS?

I believe it was the intersection of two huge movements, one of them mainly political and the other mainly demographic. The first of these, because it was strictly of its time, we can describe fairly briefly and then set aside. The second, because it is a profound and momentous change in our society that will be playing out for decades to come, will take a couple of chapters to discuss.

The Housing Bubble

The concentration of foreclosures by state—the fact that a handful of states account for such a huge proportion of the total—stems from a lot of people without a lot of money being allowed to buy homes they couldn't afford.

The national average rose from house values 2.2 times the median family income in 1990 to 2.4 in 2000 to 3.2 times in 2007. As a national average, this gap was too high: it had risen by

TABLE 1.4 2006 MEDIAN HOME SALES PRICES COMPARED TO SECOND
QUARTER 2009 TRADITIONAL HOME MEDIAN SALES
PRICES, BY MLS AREA

CODE	MLS AREA	2006 ($)	SECOND QUARTER 2009 ($)	PERCENT CHANGE 2006–2009
365	Maple Grove/Osseo	247,900	269,700	9.2
300	Minneapolis–Calhoun/Isles	263,590	287,000	8.9
368	Hennepin–Northwest	375,000	397,495	6.0
302	Minneapolis–Central	270,000	285,779	5.8
397	Chaska	234,900	248,500	5.8
396	Chanhassen	293,500	310,000	5.6
640	Shakopee	218,000	225,000	3.2
741	Saint Paul–Downtown/Capitol Heights	195,000	200,848	3.0
642	Prior Lake	279,900	287,925	2.9
610	Eagan	237,800	239,850	0.9
386	Hopkins	205,900	207,000	0.5
726	Woodbury	281,000	282,250	0.4
374	Plymouth	293,000	291,000	(0.7)
385	Edina	385,000	380,000	(1.3)

Source: Minneapolis Area Association of Realtors

33 percent in seven years. It probably was this nation's largest-ever income-to-house-value gap. Those high prices relative to income could be supported only by easy credit, with low down payments, low interest rates, and particular repayment schedules.

The foreclosure crisis was triggered in those states where house prices to income ratios widened the most. The gap was greatest in California (8.3 to 1), and that is why the foreclosure crisis was concentrated there. It was second highest in Nevada

(5.1 to 1), which had the highest foreclosure rate. Next were Arizona and Florida (4.2 to 1).

That leads to two questions. First, why did the house value to income gap increase nationally? Second, why did it increase most rapidly in California, Nevada, Arizona, and Florida? The first question is easier to answer than the second, but circumstantial evidence provides some clues to the second one.

The national average rose because two U.S. presidents and several sessions of Congress were eager to increase the rate of home ownership. That rate had been stable at 64 to 66 percent from the 1960s into the 1990s. If nothing changed, it would stay there.

President Clinton set a goal of increasing the home ownership rate to 67.5 percent. He succeeded. By 2000, the home ownership rate had climbed to 67.7 percent. President Bush sought to increase it well above that. Although he did not set a percentage goal, he advocated increasing minority home ownership by 5.5 million. With nearly 70 million owner-occupant households out of more than 105 million total households in 2000, 5.5 million more home owners would increase the ownership rate to 71.4 percent. Said President Bush in October 2002, "We want everybody in America to own their own home."[13]

Fannie Mae and Freddie Mac were encouraged to ease mortgage purchase standards. Simpler, faster, less personalized loan processing was one thing that could be made less expensive by computerizing it. These agencies also were urged to make lending to minorities easier, because home ownership among minority groups was lower than among whites.

Politicians wanted to increase home ownership in order to help people build equity and wealth. Inequalities of wealth were greater than inequalities of income. For most households, home ownership was the main means by which wealth was acquired. This occurred for two reasons. Home values increased, by and large, over time, and paying mortgages, even if house values did not increase, was a form of forced savings, yielding substantial equity when the mortgage was completely paid.

Home ownership also was seen as encouraging participation in civic life, a liberal value, and leading to resistance to taxes and support for small government, a conservative value. Moreover, the American dream, especially the suburban variant, required home ownership, which symbolized control of space, self-worth, and full standing as a citizen. It conveyed informal status, as well as stability and savings for retirement.

Clinton's support for more home ownership coincided with a period of growing income inequality. More income inequality would lead to more wealth inequality. Increasing the home ownership rate for low- and moderate-income households would reduce those wealth inequalities. As employment rose and unemployment fell, the trend to more income inequality moderated. And stable employment encouraged the hope that mortgages could be paid if down payments could be reduced. Employment was seen as a sufficient basis for a mortgage, because owning a home was seen as a way to increase savings. But if savings were required to get a mortgage, then low income households would be denied access to home ownership and would be barred from fully realizing the American dream.

For President Bush, the recession that followed the September 11, 2001, attacks created a political as well as an economic problem. While rallying around the flag of retaliation in Afghanistan and then Iraq was potent politically, the economic downtown created political vulnerability. Easy credit to promote more home ownership was necessary because of the economic downturn and slow recovery. The recovery that occurred was stimulated in substantial part by the housing boom. The housing boom in turn depended upon easy credit. Consequently, Fannie Mae and Freddie Mac were encouraged to continue and expand support for easy credit by lenders.

During this period, private entrepreneurs came up with additional methods of drawing low-income borrowers, and other borrowers in high-cost states, into home ownership. Their initiatives, however, depended upon Fannie Mae and Freddie Mac buying the mortgages created with easy credit. A new private secondary mortgage market also could advance this cause. That was where mortgage-backed securities and collateralized debt obligations came in. They created a private secondary market for mortgages that previously were purchased only by

Fannie Mae and Freddie Mac. Challenged by the private sector, Fannie Mae and Freddie Mac became even more eager to purchase risky mortgages to maintain a high level of business activity, trying to prevent losing more market share.

Politics and economics were intertwined. Increasing home ownership was a value that the Bush administration wanted to promote. This goal was potent economically, because it was the most important single fuel for economic recovery. As frustration with a long war in Iraq increased, the political importance of economic expansion increased.

Political geography also was important. Nevada, Arizona, and Florida were crucial components of the Bush coalition in 2000 and 2004. Support for home ownership increases was especially significant in those states because many low- and moderate-income Hispanics lived in those states, and their political allegiances were not firmly set. The Bush strategists thought that support for home ownership would make Hispanics more conservative. Conservative family values already had given the Bush administration reasons to hope for Hispanic support. Home ownership policies became even more important in wooing the Hispanic vote, because President Bush's hope of winning immigrant support through broad immigration reform was dashed by anxiety about immigration that followed the September 11, 2001, attacks. The importance of Hispanics in those states can be seen by comparing their Hispanic population percentage to the 12.5 percent national average in 2000—Arizona 25.2 percent, California 32.4 percent, Florida 16.8 percent, and Nevada 19.7 percent.

The last ingredient needed to expand home ownership was local lenders to initiate mortgage loans to buyers with modest to low qualifications. A new category of lenders who specialized in housing, especially subprime mortgages, was the final element added to institutional capacity. These were private firms like Countryside Financial and Washington Mutual. California was part of this mix because it had eager entrepreneurs and many low- and moderate-income Hispanics to lure into home ownership. California also had rapidly escalating housing prices that created a sort of "greater fool" paradise. As long as one "greater fool" buyer of an overpriced property could be found, prices could keep going up. With many people making quick profits on resales, the notion that suburbs and exurbs were reliable places to invest was reinforced.

Cheap credit enabled move-up buyers and first-time buyers. Young buyers wanted to be smart, investing in housing instead of wasting money on rent. They feared losing housing investment opportunities as prices kept rising. Most of them were not low income, but they were stretched, paying more than they could afford if their incomes fell. They were especially vulnerable to declines in housing prices, quickly going "under water" with mortgages exceeding home values, because they bought with little or no down payments and had paid little or no principal during the first year(s) of their mortgage. This aspect of the home ownership boom depended on outer suburban and exurban expansion, because that was where developers acquired large tracts of land and got local political support for real estate growth.

In Nevada, Arizona, and Florida, real estate growth became the main mode of economic growth. As one cheeky analyst observed, once it all started coming unglued and people started to actually begin leaving Florida, the entire state of Florida was a Ponzi scheme in which new arrivals kept paying in, which kept the costs for others down. "Everything is fine for me if a thousand newcomers come tomorrow," said one owner.[14] Prosperity in those states depended on easy credit for housing. Political prospects for holding on to those states for the Republican Party in 2004, 2006, and 2008 were much greater if housing-fueled prosperity continued. Democrats were pleased to go along, because they wanted to raise home ownership for minorities. These political and economic entanglements blew apart with full fury in the foreclosure crisis of 2008 and 2009.

This account is not intended to hold Alan Greenspan, the Federal Reserve Board, and the regulators of housing and financial markets harmless from blame. They were immersed in the virtues, as they saw them, of deregulation of financial institutions, another goal promoted by the Bush administration. Had Greenspan and the regulators at the Securities and Exchange

Commission reined in the more adventurous financial instruments, the global financial crisis would have been less cataclysmic. But they would have been swimming upstream against a tide of public policy promoting home ownership that was supported both by the Republican president and the Democratic Congress. A political crisis would have occurred. Neither Greenspan's economic philosophy nor political acumen recommended such a confrontation.

As fingers of blame were pointed in several directions, coming to rest most often on the financial market regulators, the greedy lenders, and the witless manipulators of mortgage-backed securities, the elected officials occasionally pointed at one another, focusing on the failure to require more effective oversight of financial markets.

None of the elected officials pointed at the policy of increasing the home ownership rate to a height that could be supported only by cheap credit and lax lending. When the recession winds down, financial institutions are stabilized, and business as usual achieves a comeback, the most important questions will remain: What should the nation's home ownership goal be, and which policies can safely be designed to pursue it?

But something else was also afoot—and had been afoot, though few were noticing, for quite a number of years. The whole pattern of metropolitan development was quietly moving in reverse.

NOTES

1. Lora Pabst, "Empty Houses: Whose Job Is It to Watch Them?" Minneapolis *StarTribune*, March 17, 2009.
2. Christopher Snowbeck, "Homeowners Leave It All After a Foreclosure, and Someone Has to Clean It Up," St. Paul *Pioneer Press*, September 13, 2009.
3. Paul Donsky, "Volume of 'Subdivision' Vacant Lots Overwhelms Banks," *Atlanta Journal-Constitution*, August 9, 2009.
4. Jennifer Steinhauer, "A Cul-de-sac of Lost Dreams, and New Ones," *New York Times*, August 22, 2009.
5. Data for 236 counties in 35 metropolitan areas are in Appendix 1.
6. Henry J. Cordes, "Foreclosures May Be Right Around the Corner," *Omaha World-Herald*, August 9, 2009.

7. Nick Miroff, "Foreclosure Auctioneers' Lonely Task," *Washington Post*, February 27, 2008.

8. Peter Y. Hong, "Some Home Prices Crater to 80s Levels," *Los Angeles Times*, June 10, 2009.

9. Amy Gardner, "Fairfax Prepares to Raise Tax Rate as Region's Fiscal Outlook Darkens," *Washington Post*, April 22, 2008.

10. Alejandro Lazo, "A Trying Year, By The Numbers," *Washington Post*, March 28, 2009.

11. See www.activerain.com.

12. James B. McComb, "McComb Group Ltd., Housing Market Review" (McComb Group, Minneapolis), July 28, 2009.

13. Niall Ferguson, *The Ascent of Money: A Financial History of the World* (New York: Penguin Press, 2008).

14. George Packer, "A Reporter at Large: The Ponzi State," *The New Yorker*, February 9, 2009.

What Income Reveals

When the results of the 1990 Census began to emerge, the *Washington Post* pronounced them troubling.

> For many of the nation's big cities, the preliminary 1990 census figures tell a depressing story: greater than expected population losses that will result in a weakened political base and, for those who remain behind, increasingly grim and isolated social conditions.
>
> In Chicago, for example, the census reported population declines of more than 9 percent since 1980, a trend tied to a devastating loss of manufacturing jobs. More than 60 percent of the remaining population is minority, with 40 percent of families living in poverty in many inner-city neighborhoods.[1]

That was then, and remains to a large extent today, *the* standard litany of urban decline. People (understood in these contexts to mean white people) are leaving for nicer, leafier, newer places. Left behind are the poor and minorities—often the same folks—increasingly isolated from cheerful prosperity and without the wherewithal to maintain, much less improve, their grim surroundings. General statements about the ailing city are punctuating by telling, not to say stunning and depressing, details, such the one conveyed by this page-one headline:

In One Home, a Mighty City's Rise and Fall: Price of Typical Detroit House: \$7,100[2]

In reality, however, that 1990 Census was already signaling what has become more and more evident with each passing year. A turnaround is under way in the fortunes of cities, even as the prospects for suburbs have grown more and more uncertain. Let's go back to the 1980s and take this process decade by decade.

1980s

The 1990 Census found that a number of cities that had been losing population for decades were now stabilizing: not gaining much, but no longer losing. Minneapolis, for instance, was still "losing," but take a look at the extent of the losses compared to those of earlier decades (Fig. 2.1). After losing 150,000 people over three census cycles, owing mainly to households becoming smaller and smaller as the four- or eight-child 1950s home became a thing of the past, it had become essentially stable. Given the census's chronic problems with minority undercounts, it might not have lost at all.

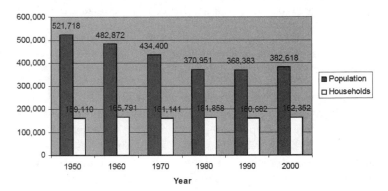

Minneapolis City Council, *The Minneapolis Plan for Sustainable Growth*, October 2, 2009, chap. 3, p. 2.

Figure 2.1 Population and Number of Households, Minneapolis, 1950–2000

Conversely, much of the *population* stability of a city like Minneapolis during the 1980s stemmed from its attractiveness to job-hungry minority refugees from steel mills in cities like Chicago and Gary, Indiana. Big American cities during the 1980s were becoming less prosperous: per capita incomes were still dropping. But that situation was about to change.

1990s

During the 1990s, something remarkable began to happen. Cities were attracting people with money. Some were succeeding at this more than others, of course. But even across the full spectrum of our biggest cities—specifically, the 40 central cities in the 35 most populous metropolitan areas as of 1980—the decline in average per capita income that had lasted through the 1980s stopped.

That shift is doubly remarkable because it was taking place even as millions of poverty-stricken immigrants, arriving in this country from Latin American nations during the 1990s, were taking up residence in these same cities. Generally speaking, they were pulling averages down; so someone else was doing double duty in pulling them up. This change in the statistics was being driven by a new attractiveness of cities to affluent whites.

In the 40 cities by the year 2000, the per capita income of non-Hispanic whites was, on average, 5 percent higher than that of their metropolitan areas as a whole (see Table 2.1). That wasn't equally true, of course, in every place. It wasn't true at all in Detroit, where affluent whites had indeed fled to the suburbs: the per capita income of non-Hispanic whites in that city was 34 percent less than that of their counterparts throughout the metro area. But it was emphatically true in other places, including Atlanta. The per capita income of non-Hispanic whites in that city was 73 percent higher than it was in the metro as a whole.

The revival of interest in cities on the part of middle-class whites had a lot to do with a fondness for older homes. And this represented a change. In the past, the older the home, the more likely some poor person was living in it. But now that pattern

TABLE 2.1 RELATIVE PER CAPITA INCOME OF NON-HISPANIC WHITES
IN PRINCIPAL CITIES COMPARED TO THEIR METROPOLITAN
INCOME IN 2000, 2006, 2007, AND 2008

PRINCIPAL CITY AS PERCENT OF METROPOLITAN AREA				
				Percent Difference
Principal City	2000	2006	2007	2008	2000–2008
Atlanta	173	173	181	177	4
Baltimore	89	88	90	93	4
Boston	102	113	111	112	10
Buffalo	83	92	93	86	3
Charlotte	134	129	129	130	-4
Chicago	108	120	124	122	14
Cincinnati	105	108	117	—	12
Cleveland	75	75	73	73	-2
Columbus	93	89	90	91	-2
Dallas	127	136	146	143	16
Denver	110	110	113	112	2
Detroit	66	59	63	65	-1
Houston	118	126	130	130	12
Indianapolis	99	94	98	98	-1
Kansas City	100	103	100	108	8
Las Vegas	109	107	102	101	-8
Los Angeles	110	104	108	109	-1
Miami	114	130	134	146	32
Milwaukee	83	85	82	82	-1
Minneapolis	103	105	109	106	3
New York	107	108	108	110	3
Newport News	91	87	83	92	1
Norfolk	96	99	96	98	2
Oakland	97	102	102	100	3
Orlando	116	114	124	114	-2

TABLE 2.1 (CONTINUED)

PRINCIPAL CITY AS PERCENT OF METROPOLITAN AREA				
				Percent Difference
Principal City	2000	2006	2007	2008	2000–2008
Philadelphia	79	80	81	79	0
Phoenix	100	102	101	105	5
Pittsburgh	101	99	99	108	7
Portland	101	105	101	106	5
Sacramento	100	100	106	104	4
San Antonio	102	100	102	103	1
San Diego	110	108	110	112	2
San Francisco	120	121	124	128	8
Seattle	118	122	125	125	7
St. Louis	88	—	—	95	7
St. Paul	90	92	91	96	6
St. Petersburg	101	101	100	—	-1
Tampa	124	144	137	136	12
Virginia Beach	106	106	106	106	0
Washington, D.C.	147	136	138	141	-6
Averages	105	107	108	109	4

100 percent means that per capita income in the principal city was the same as in its entire metropolitan area, including the principal city. Any percentage less than 100 means that per capita income in the principal city was less than in its entire metropolitan area. Any percentage greater than 100 means that per capita income was higher in the principal city than in its metropolitan area.

Source: Data for 2000 are from the U.S. Census of Population and Housing, Table P1571: Per Capita Income (White Alone, Not Hispanic or Latino); Data for 2006, 2007, and 2008 are from the American Community Survey, Table B19301H: Per Capita Income in the Past 12 Months (White Alone, Not Hispanic or Latino).

was shifting. Neighborhoods—technically speaking, "census tracts"—with significant numbers of homes built before 1940 were the strongest performers within big cities. They tended to see increases in family income between 1990 and 2000.[3]

Thousands of news articles and home-section features during that period touted the virtues of golden oak flooring, built-in hutches with beveled mirrors, and, more spiritually speaking, a sense of character and solidity: a feeling of having been crafted by hand, rather than slapped together by the hundreds by some national home building chain, and having been for generations the repository of family memories.

And this new trend began showing up in terms of the rising value of homes. In St. Paul, for instance, in a neighborhood near downtown that had once been home to, or associated with, such African American eminences as Dave Winfield, the baseball star, and August Wilson, the playwright, a reporter—writing in 2003, but relying on changes that had taken place in large part during the 1990s—noted:

> Market conditions in real estate have changed so dramatically in the southern half of the old Rondo neighborhood that a dilapidated crack house being refurbished is on the verge of selling for $279,000. In February 2000, the same Victorian-style residence at 836 Iglehart Av. sold for a mere $77,914. . . .
>
> Census data confirm that the racial balance has shifted away from a black majority. . . . In 1990, 51 percent of residents in that area were black and 34 percent were white. In 2000, the black population declined to 39 percent of the neighborhood, which became 42 percent white.[4]

Existing inhabitants saw it as a case of their own hard work to clean up crime creating conditions for others to invade and snatch up beautifully built homes. A black woman, a lifelong resident of the area who became president of a nonprofit working to revive the area, told a journalist that she and others resented affluent whites coming in.

> "They are the ones buying up those houses at those ridiculous prices because they can afford them," said [Zula] Young. "It's an invasion of our space, so to speak."

At the same time, there were signs of suburban frailty. Postwar suburbs were entering middle age. An analysis of 2,586 suburbs in these same 35 large metropolitan areas from 1980 to 2000 found that:[5]

- Half of those that increased in population decreased in income relative to their own metro areas.
- Concentrated poverty nearly doubled—even as concentrated poverty in central cities was dissipating.[6] The number of suburbs below 80 percent of the metropolitan median family income was four times higher in 1990 than it had been in 1960.
- It wasn't just the inner-ring suburb that was weakening. Some places 20 to 40 miles from the central city declined in relative income, a sign that as home prices rose, poorer people were driving farther and farther in quest of affordable homes.
- Overall, 52 percent of suburbs were declining faster or increasing more slowly than their central cities in relative per capita income, as were 33 percent in relative median family income.

In fact, in 155 suburbs, per capita income was less than 60 percent of metropolitan per capita income, meaning that, in their own metropolitan contexts, they were worse off than Detroit, which was the lowest-income central city relative to its metropolitan area in 2000. The 1990 census had found just 121 suburbs in that category.

2000s

Since 2000, central cities have done even better. By 2008, central cities were not just stabilizing when it came to per capita income. They were rising. (See Table 2.2.) From incomes at 88 percent of the metro-wide figure in 2000, they were up to 91 percent. And this again understated the success of most, while masking the struggles of others. Between 2006 and 2007, per capita income ratios increased in 21 cities, stayed the same in seven, and went down in 12. Then, between 2007 and 2008, they increased in 20 cities, stayed the same in seven, and declined in 13.

There continued to be signs of affluence among whites in central cities. By 2008, the per capita income of non-Hispanic whites was 9 percent higher than their metropolitan areas (Table 2.3). Atlanta led in this department: whites were 77 percent

TABLE 2.2 PERCENT CITY INCOME RELATIVE TO METROPOLITAN INCOME, 1980 TO 2008

RELATIVE PER CAPITA INCOME						
Principal City	1980	1990	2000	2006	2007	2008
Atlanta	84	90	103	115	125	118
Baltimore	77	72	70	68	68	69
Boston	80	81	80	88	88	88
Buffalo	84	77	74	75	76	75
Charlotte	107	115	115	110	110	110
Chicago	81	78	81	86	89	88
Cincinnati	92	87	87	85	89	86
Cleveland	72	63	64	63	62	61
Columbus	91	91	89	83	83	83
Dallas	104	99	91	92	95	93
Denver	96	94	92	90	94	94
Detroit	73	60	60	53	56	54
Houston	99	95	92	92	96	95
Indianapolis	98	96	93	86	90	89
Kansas City	92	92	89	90	88	94
Las Vegas	98	98	104	100	99	99
Los Angeles	101	96	95	93	95	96
Miami	79	72	82	82	73	80
Milwaukee	85	75	70	68	65	68
Minneapolis	92	88	87	89	94	91
New York	88	86	84	87	88	89
Newport News	103	94	88	87	83	89
Norfolk	91	86	85	85	84	84
Oakland	80	73	69	72	77	75
Orlando	95	93	100	98	102	97
Philadelphia	81	74	69	67	68	66
Phoenix	98	94	91	89	88	90

TABLE 2.2 (CONTINUED)

RELATIVE PER CAPITA INCOME						
Principal City	1980	1990	2000	2006	2007	2008
Pittsburgh	89	90	90	87	88	95
Portland	97	96	97	101	99	103
Sacramento	96	91	84	87	89	89
San Antonio	92	92	94	93	93	94
San Diego	101	101	103	104	106	107
San Francisco	97	97	109	114	116	117
Seattle	100	102	109	115	119	122
St. Louis	77	72	71	72	72	75
St. Paul	89	82	77	77	77	80
St. Petersburg	99	98	97	97	95	103
Tampa	91	92	101	111	106	107
Virginia Beach	115	113	110	111	109	112
Washington, D.C.	87	88	94	96	99	100
Average of 40	91	88	88	89	90	91

100 percent means that income in the principal city was the same as in its entire metropolitan area, including the principal city. Any percentage less than 100 means that income in the principal city was less than its entire metropolitan area. Any percentage greater than 100 means that income was higher in the principal city than in its metropolitan area.

Source: Data for 1980 through 2000 are from the Census of Population and Housing. Data for 2006, 2007 and 2008 are from the American Community Survey, Table B19301.

higher. Dallas was 43 percent higher, Washington, D.C., 41, and Tampa 36. Seven northeast and Midwest cities had higher per capita incomes for non-Hispanic whites than their suburbs in 2007 or 2008: Boston (12 percent higher), Chicago (22 percent), Cincinnati (17 percent), Kansas City (8 percent), Minneapolis (6 percent), New York (10 percent), and Pittsburgh (8 percent).

At the same time, more affluent minorities were heading out to the suburbs. By 2006, per capita incomes for blacks, Hispanics, and Asians were higher outside the central cities than in. In other words, there was more evidence of black flight to the suburbs, Hispanic flight, and Asian flight than of white flight.

TABLE 2.3 PER CAPITA INCOME IN PRINCIPAL CITIES RELATIVE TO EACH METROPOLITAN AREA'S INCOME IN 2006

Principal City	PERCENTAGE OF PRINCIPAL CITY TO METROPOLITAN AREA INCOME					
	All	White	Black	Hispanic	White Non-Hispanic	Asian
Atlanta	115	173	81	123	173	90
Baltimore	68	89	78	67	88	95
Boston	88	108	92	63	113	100
Buffalo	75	89	99	45	92	84
Charlotte	110	125	105	105	129	104
Chicago	86	115	93	89	120	93
Cincinnati	85	108	85	81	108	106
Cleveland	63	74	82	57	75	76
Columbus	83	88	95	79	89	92
Dallas	92	107	84	123	136	88
Denver	90	98	88	103	110	82
Detroit	53	56	84	37	59	71
Houston	92	102	89	92	126	91
Indianapolis	86	93	94	69	94	86
Kansas City	90	102	93	68	103	97
Las Vegas	100	103	92	106	107	91
Los Angeles	93	99	94	95	104	88
Miami	82	84	73	73	130	79
Milwaukee	68	83	94	61	85	87
Minneapolis	89	102	88	66	105	100
New York	87	102	92	79	108	91
Newport News	87	87	100	111	87	90
Norfolk	85	100	78	68	99	104
Oakland	72	91	93	69	102	71

TABLE 2.3 (CONTINUED)

Principal City	PERCENTAGE OF PRINCIPAL CITY TO METROPOLITAN AREA INCOME					
	All	White	Black	Hispanic	White Non-Hispanic	Asian
Orlando	98	110	87	94	114	100
Philadelphia	67	78	82	66	80	78
Phoenix	89	90	91	92	102	89
Pittsburgh	87	99	83	65	99	72
Portland	101	105	86	81	105	104
Sacramento	87	93	91	93	100	90
San Antonio	93	94	98	108	100	99
San Diego	104	107	96	97	108	103
San Francisco	114	120	89	94	121	126
Seattle	115	124	90	91	122	123
St. Louis	72	89	80	77	—	—
St. Paul	77	90	73	54	92	77
St. Petersburg	97	104	83	96	101	111
Tampa	111	127	82	83	144	115
Virginia Beach	111	105	114	95	106	99
Washington, D.C.	96	137	78	133	136	121
Averages	89	101	89	84	107	94

100 Percent means that per capita income in the principal city was the same as in its entire metropolitan area, including the principal city in 2006. Any percentage less than 100 means that per capita income in the principal city was less than in its entire metropolitan area. Any percentage greater than 100 means that per capita income was higher in the principal city than in its metropolitan area.

Source: American Community Survey: Computed from Tables B19301 and A, B, D, H & I. Per Capita Income in the Past 12 Months by Race.

In short, affluent whites and affluent minorities seemed to be trading places. Blacks' per capita income in cities declined from 92 percent of metropolitan income in 2000 to 89 percent in 2006. Only 10 cities showed increases. By 2006, blacks had higher incomes in cities than in their suburbs only in Virginia Beach and Charlotte. In contrast, per capita incomes of non-Hispanic whites were higher in 27 cities than their suburbs in 2006.

The value of homes in cities was rising. In 2000, in the 40 cities, the median value of owner-occupied homes stood at 87 percent of that of their metropolitan areas. By 2006, the figure was up to 90 percent; by 2007, 91 percent; and by 2008, 92 percent (Table 2.4).

One reason these relatively subtle signs of urban rebound are not widely known is that they have not always coincided with increases in the populations of these same groups—an indicator that has always been treated in our popular culture, and will likely long remain, as the number-one vital sign of the health of cities and states.

If anything, it has looked as if minorities—or at any rate, the largest group among them—continue to stream into cities. The Hispanic share of city populations increased 2.2 percent from 2000 to 2005.[7] Hispanics' population share increased in 36 of 40 cities from 2000 to 2005.[8]

During that time, non-Hispanic whites declined in numbers, just by a whisker: by 0.4 percent. But their numbers were still shrinking. And if they are still *leaving*, a skeptic may ask, then what really has changed? How can one speak of an urban rebound?

The answer is that the number of white *households* was rising in many places, as condo towers went up, but even that couldn't entirely offset the powerful demographic forces of aging.

Imagine a typical city block in south Minneapolis. Between 2000 and 2005, let's say that two elderly white widows pass away and another down the street becomes a widow when her husband dies. A Hispanic family buys one of the newly empty homes, and a childless white couple buys another. A few other homes are occupied by white Baby Boomer couples whose children graduate from high school and leave home, oftentimes departing the state altogether, for universities in Madison or Boulder or Iowa City, or perhaps to join the army.

TABLE 2.4 MEDIAN VALUE OWNER-OCCUPIED HOUSING IN PRINCIPAL CITIES RELATIVE TO METROPOLITAN AREAS, 2000, 2006, 2007, AND 2008

PRINCIPAL CITY	2000 CITY AS PERCENT OF METRO AREA	2006 CITY AS PERCENT OF METRO AREA	2007 CITY AS PERCENT OF METRO AREA	2008 CITY AS PERCENT OF METRO AREA	PERCENT DIFFERENCE IN CITY TO METRO AREA 2000–2008
Atlanta	109	125	123	128	19
Baltimore	53	42	51	55	2
Boston	92	108	107	104	12
Buffalo	68	58	56	58	-10
Charlotte	113	104	105	105	-8
Chicago	89	110	110	107	18
Cincinnati	84	81	85	84	0
Cleveland	61	60	59	57	-4
Columbus	83	86	85	86	3
Dallas	86	87	88	85	-1
Denver	84	96	96	98	14
Detroit	49	53	52	50	1
Houston	90	92	91	93	3
Indianapolis	88	88	87	85	-3
Kansas City	80	85	85	85	5
Las Vegas	106	97	98	98	-8
Los Angeles	107	102	103	104	-3
Miami	103	102	107	114	11
Milwaukee	61	69	71	70	9
Minneapolis	82	95	95	96	14
New York	96	108	115	118	22
Newport News	88	77	80	84	-4

TABLE 2.4 (CONTINUED)

PRINCIPAL CITY	2000 CITY AS PERCENT OF METRO AREA	2006 CITY AS PERCENT OF METRO AREA	2007 CITY AS PERCENT OF METRO AREA	2008 CITY AS PERCENT OF METRO AREA	PERCENT DIFFERENCE IN CITY TO METRO AREA 2000–2008
Norfolk	82	82	84	85	3
Oakland	67	84	84	80	13
Orlando	98	98	103	101	3
Philadelphia	51	50	57	55	3
Phoenix	89	92	95	96	7
Pittsburgh	72	69	73	72	0
Portland	93	99	99	101	8
Sacramento	81	86	88	84	3
San Antonio	91	91	89	91	0
San Diego	104	101	100	105	1
San Francisco	124	115	118	122	-2
Seattle	129	120	126	129	0
St. Louis	66	77	81	78	12
St. Paul	75	87	88	85	10
St. Petersburg	92	97	94	98	6
Tampa	95	102	110	113	18
Virginia Beach	113	116	118	112	1
Washington, D.C.	89	96	98	110	21
Averages	87	90	91	92	5

Source: Data for 2000 are from the U.S. Census of Population and Housing, Table H85: Median Value All Owner Occupied Housing. Data for 2006, 2007, and 2008 are from the American Community Survey, Table B25077: Median Value Owner Occupied Housing.

The white population has declined, yes. But none of these folks is part of any stereotypical white-flight exodus to the suburbs.

At the southern edge of downtown Minneapolis, during these same five years, developers were building a 27-story tower called Grant Park, with 39 townhomes and 288 condominiums. On a single city block, in other words, they installed as many new housing units as some fairly robust high-growth suburbs will add, over far more acreage, in an entire year.

This, in microcosm, is what has happened in many cities. A study of the 50 largest metro areas between 1990 and 2007 found that

> in roughly half of the metropolitan areas examined, urban core communities dramatically increased their share of new residential building permits. . . . In fifteen regions, the central city more than doubled its share of permits. . . . The increase has been particularly dramatic over the past five years. Data from 2007 show the shift inward continuing in the wake of the real estate market downturn.[9]

Between the early 1990s and the six years from 2001 to 2007, New York City's share of regional building permits increased from 15 percent to 44 percent. Chicago went from 7 percent to 23 percent. Portland rose from 9 percent to 22 percent. Atlanta grew from 4 percent to 13 percent.

As recently as the 1990s in Minneapolis–St. Paul, the private consulting industry gathering building-permit statistics for the local home builders' group didn't even bother to check to see whether any building activity was going on in the two central cities. It was assumed that central cities lost housing units through the demolition of vacant ones in poor neighborhoods; they didn't actually add them. But by the first decade of the 21st century, the two central cities were often the leading location of new building units (Fig. 2.2).

And it was crucial to look at who was buying them. When a city such as Oakland aspires to increase its downtown population by 10,000 it's clear what is meant. American cities had long had, at least at the fringes of their central business districts, plenty of people "living downtown"—many of them in cheap

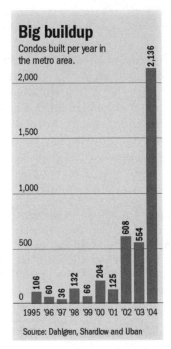

From Terry Fiedler, "The New Land Rush," Minneapolis *StarTribune*,
April 17, 2005, p. 1A.

Figure 2.2 Condos Built Per Year, Minneapolis–St. Paul, 1995–2004

hotels, homeless shelters, drug treatment centers, jails, and
exceptionally grim apartment buildings. The call for 10,000
people does not refer to any eagerness in Oakland to increase
the number of people in any of these categories. So when analysts of downtown revival seek to document that revival, they
find that they cannot really capture what is going on by simply
counting up the number of people. They need to look further
than that, to the *sort* of people who are living downtown. That's
why experts develop charts like Figure 2.3.[10]

The affluence of condominium owners helped drive income
increases in some cities after 2000. In the 40 cities analyzed
in this book, condominium ownership—owner occupancy of
structures with five or more units—increased from 6.1 percent

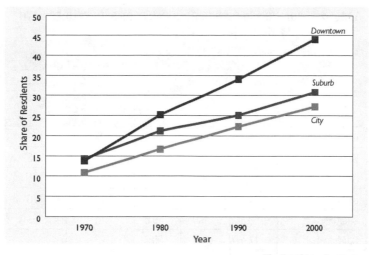

The Brookings Institution

Figure 2.3 Change in Share of Residents with a Bachelor's Degree, 1970–2000

in 2000 to 7.2 percent in 2005. Between 2000 and 2007, condominium shares increased in all 40 cities. The largest increase occurred from 2005 to 2007, when it went to 11.8 percent, a 93 percent increase from 2000 (Table 2.5).[11]

One of the main things that had turned middle-class Americans off about cities, of course, was the danger posed by crime. But by 2008 and 2009, journalists were filing puzzled reports that, even amid horrendous economic conditions, crime was dropping in many cities:

- "Fewer Murders on City Streets," San Francisco *Examiner*, June 2, 2009
- "Crime Drops in L.A., Defying Experts," *Los Angeles Times*, April 1, 2009
- "Crime Soars in the 'Burbs," [Trenton, N.J.] *Trentonian*, January 25, 2009
- "Violent Crime Declines in City," *Philadelphia Inquirer*, December 31, 2008

TABLE 2.5 CHANGES IN OWNER OCCUPANCY OF STRUCTURES WITH 5 OR MORE UNITS, 2000–2007

Principal City	OCCUPIED 5+ UNIT STRUCTURES, OWNER-OCCUPIED			PERCENT CHANGE	
	2000 (%)	2005 (%)	2007 (%)	2000–2005	2000–2007
Atlanta	9.8	18.8	23.4	92	139
Baltimore	2.9	3.4	9.5	17	228
Boston	19.6	21.8	22.5	11	15
Buffalo	1	1.3	4.7	28	370
Charlotte	3.8	4.0	9.6	4	153
Chicago	17.4	21.4	30.3	23	74
Cincinnati	3.3	3.6	7.2	7	118
Cleveland	1.1	1.3	3.3	21	200
Columbus	2.8	2.6	6.0	-7	114
Dallas	3.9	5.2	6.7	33	72
Denver	11.1	12.7	22.9	14	106
Detroit	1.2	1.3	4.1	13	242
Houston	4.4	5.3	5.9	21	34
Indianapolis	0.9	1.0	4.8	8	433
Kansas City	1.4	1.6	6.2	13	343
Las Vegas	2.5	2.6	7.3	1	192
Los Angeles	8.4	8.7	8.7	4	4
Miami	18.9	21.9	20.2	15	7
Milwaukee	3.0	3.2	9.6	6	220
Minneapolis	5.9	7.2	13.2	21	124
New York	14.4	16.4	17.2	14	19
Newport News	2.6	2.7	5.4	2	108
Norfolk	3.7	2.9	6.5	-21	75

TABLE 2.5 (CONTINUED)

Principal City	OCCUPIED 5+ UNIT STRUCTURES, OWNER-OCCUPIED			PERCENT CHANGE	
	2000 (%)	2005 (%)	2007 (%)	2000–2005	2000–2007
Phoenix	2.0	2.3	8.0	16	300
Pittsburgh	3.4	4.1	8.9	20	162
Portland	2.5	3.2	10.4	29	316
Sacramento	0.7	1.0	3.3	42	371
San Antonio	1.2	1.1	3.1	-12	158
San Diego	8.1	10.0	17.8	23	120
San Francisco	11.0	12.9	12.2	17	11
Seattle	11.2	14.1	16.8	25	50
St. Louis	2.4	3.0	8.7	24	263
St. Paul	3.8	4.7	10.3	24	171
St. Petersburg	9.7	12.5	26.3	29	171
Tampa	4.3	5.1	14.7	17	242
Virginia Beach	3.1	3.9	17.2	24	455
Washington, D.C.	17.9	21.0	22.2	17	24
Averages	6.1	7.2	11.8	18	93

Source: Data for 2000 are from the U.S. Census of Population and Housing, Table H32: Tenure by Housing Units. Data for 2005 and 2007 are from the American Community Survey, Table B25032: Tenure by Housing Units.

- "Killings Fall in L.A., Rise in Valley: Local Surge an Anomaly as City Levels at Lowest Point since 1969," Los Angeles *Daily News*, January 2, 2009
- "City Homicides at 23-year Low," *Baltimore Sun*, April 7, 2008
- "Murder Down 6.5% in Big Cities," *USA Today*, January 8, 2008

The historic comparisons were striking:

> The District, New York and Los Angeles are on track for fewer kill-
> ings this year [2009] than in any other year in at least four decades.
> Boston, San Francisco, Minneapolis and other cities are also seeing
> notable reductions in homicides. . . . The District is on track to have
> fewer killings than in any year since 1964, when the population
> was about 760,000. . . . In 1991, the District was known as the mur-
> der capital of the United States, recording 479 that year. This year,
> there have been 79.[12]

> The homicide rate in Minneapolis is at a near 25-year low, with
> only six killings recorded in the city in the first part of the year.
> "That is truly remarkable," said Chuck Wexler, executive director
> of the Police Executive Research Forum in Washington, D.C., who
> helped Minneapolis formulate its juvenile crime plan. "That's a far
> cry from the [mid-]1990s when it was known as Murderapolis."[13]

By the end of the decade, Census Bureau annual estimates
were finally beginning to show hints of a consistent rebound
in population in the nation's biggest cities—always and inevitably the bottom line in any conventional analysis. The Brookings Institution compiled the summary in Figure 2.4.

Brookings also developed the comparison with suburbs
shown in Figure 2.5.[14]

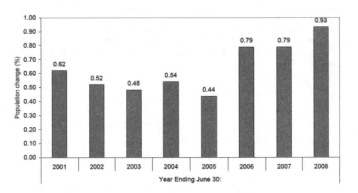

The Brookings Institution

*Figure 2.4 Annual Growth Rates, 2000–2008, U.S. Cities with
Populations over 1 Million*

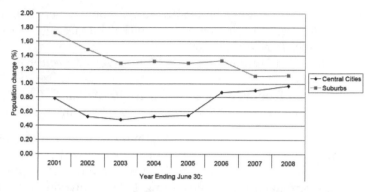

The Brookings Institution

Figure 2.5 Annual Central City versus Suburban Growth, 2000–2008, Metro Areas over 1 Million Population

None of this is to deny that there's such a thing as white flight. Many big-city school districts still have problems. On that mythical city block in south Minneapolis, some young couple with children nearing kindergarten age, anxious about the reputation of city schools, anxious about their childrens' safety as the kids grew more independent, was no doubt moving to the suburbs, in the classic "white flight" scenario.

But the numbers suggest that this is no longer the dominant suburban paradigm. And that's partly because people can tell that suburbs are changing.

In the 'burbs, the elderly became more numerous. Immigrants and minorities moved in. Most of those responsible, in fact, for the immense national increase in immigrants during the 1990s moved first to suburbs rather than cities. Schools in suburbs today are more diverse, with more students eligible for free and reduced lunches and more needing language assistance. Suburbs with more elderly people face challenges when it comes to transporting them and keeping them healthy.

- "City Pupils' Scores Rising: . . . Baltimore Children Outperform Some Suburban Peers in Math, Reading," *Baltimore Sun*, July 22, 2009

- "Subdivisions Fight a Slide into Slums: Homeowners Blame Foreclosures as Their Neighborhoods Fall into Decay," *Houston Chronicle*, March 29, 2009
- "Denver Gets Whiter; Suburbs More Diverse," *Denver Post*, March 29, 2009
- "Diversity Blooms in Outer Suburbs: Pr. William's Growth Spurred by Minorities," *Washington Post*, November 3, 2008

Suburbs, in short, are looking a lot more like the stereotypical image of cities, even as some of the wealthiest people in some of the toniest suburbs in the area around Minneapolis were decamping from estates along Lake Minnetonka, way out in the suburbs, for riverside condominiums alongside new theaters and new performance spaces and new parks and new farmers markets and restaurants and wine bars and coffee shops along the Mississippi River.

To summarize: After 2000, the revival of cities intensified. It was now visible in citywide statistics pertaining to income and the value of homes and even, eventually, in population estimates. Middle-aged suburban decline continued but was obscured by the run-up in housing prices from 2002 to 2006, nurtured by easy credit and by rapid population increases in exurbia.

But this exurban land rush was about to flame out as easy credit dried up. Seemingly so powerful for so many years, it turned out to be surprisingly vulnerable to changed conditions. Foreclosures ramped up rapidly—not mainly in cities and older suburbs, as many news accounts implied. In reality, foreclosures and their lost dreams were concentrated in new suburbs and exurbs.

Suddenly, in other words, the geography of the American home ownership dream had reversed direction. The outer suburbs, which had seemed the safest housing investment, became the burial ground of wasted dreams.

Yet the standard litany of urban decline was so powerfully ingrained by now in the psyche of analysts and interpreters of American life that even the Census Bureau's reports that *populations* of big cities were reviving was treated not as a sign of their success but as a sign that the flameout in suburban home buying was preventing the customary suburban flight. The

Associated Press, the most widely circulated news service in the nation, reported not as interpretation but as fact the claim that growth in central cities was proof that "the economic crisis is making it harder for people to move."[15]

One reason for skepticism at that moment in urban history, it seems safe to suggest, was the bloodbath taking place in the center of town. This book has mentioned a "ring of death" surrounding our metropolitan areas by the end of the first decade of the 21st century: unfinished homes, empty lots, raging weeds. But there is a parallel reality: the dark tower at the center of town.

Even as the residents of new subdivisions at the fringe gazed out at acres of windblown dirt, the residents of many condominium towers downtown found themselves just about as lonely. Gleaming new skyscrapers stood half-empty—or more than half. In Seattle, it was building after building after building:[16]

- Bellevue Towers: 184 of 539 units presold, but only 43 have closed.
- Enso: 136 units; no closings. . . .
- Fifteen Twenty-One Second Avenue: 82 of 143 units closed.
- Four Seasons Private Residences: 22 of 36 units closed, none since February.
- Olive 8: 28 of 229 units closed.
- Washington Square: 171 of 379 units closed.

In Oakland, 10 years after City Hall had launched its cleverly named 10K program—its attempt to lure 10,000 new residents downtown—the reality was closer to 5K, with "hundreds of units empty, more than a dozen projects on hold and major investors hesitant to gamble on the city anytime soon"— not to mention urban pioneers questioning their decisions to invest. Many were stuck with what a journalist from neighboring San Francisco described as "expensive new homes next to the grimmer realities of Oakland life." A developer called it a "bloodbath."[17]

In Atlanta, people were asking whether the whole dream of "live, work, play"—major new projects combining condo towers with offices, movie theaters, restaurants—was dead. The success of the "massive 1997 plan unveiled for the Atlantic Steel plant, today known as Atlantic Station," with its "condos, a hotel, retail, office space, the works," led to a period during which "'mini-Atlantic Stations' were being proposed all over the metro area. . . . But now a depressed economy has derailed the train, and many wonder how, or if, it will get back on track."[18]

Perhaps the single most arresting sight was an image of a brand-new condominium tower in Florida with but one set of windows lit in the evening. In Fort Myers, a 32-story tower had been left with one tenant. Marble floors, opulent furnishings—but a dry fountain in front and a creepy silence inside. The only occupant, describing nights spent with cell phones at the ready, in case of strange sounds, said it was "almost like a scary movie."[19]

Given the spookiness not only at the outer edge of town but at its center as well, who knows which one has the best prospects for the future? That is the topic of the next chapter.

NOTES

1. Barbara Vobejda, "For Big Cities, Disheartening Census News; D.C., Chicago, Detroit Among Those Showing Greater Than Expected Population Losses," *Washington Post*, September 14, 1990.
2. Michael M. Phillips, "In One Home, a Mighty City's Rise and Fall: Price of Typical Detroit House: $7,100," *Wall Street Journal*, September 26, 2009.
3. William H. Lucy and David L. Phillips, *Tomorrow's Cities, Tomorrow's Suburbs* (Chicago: APA Planners Press, 2006).
4. Tony Kennedy, "Area Is Reborn, but for Whom? Success of Selby Av. Pleases, and Worries, Neighbors," Minneapolis *StarTribune*, July 19, 2003.
5. "Suburb," here, is a somewhat loose term that means cities located within counties that are contained within officially defined "metropolitan areas." Some of these towns would be horrified to be classed as "suburbs," as they consider themselves small rural communities far from the city. Nevertheless, they tend to be— though they are certainly not all—commuter bases.

6. Paul A. Jargowsky, *Stunning Progress, Hidden Problems: The Dramatic Decline of Concentrated Poverty in the 1990s* (Washington, D.C.: Brookings Institution, 2003).
7. Asians were up 0.6 percent. Blacks were down 0.3 percent.
8. Whites increased in 17 cities, but this category included Hispanics. Blacks increased in 18 cities, and Asians in 34. (See Table 2.3.)
9. John V. Thomas, *Residential Construction Trends in America's Metropolitan Regions* (Washington, D.C.: U.S. Environmental Protection Agency, 2009).
10. Eugenie L. Birch, *Who Lives Downtown?* (Washington, D.C.: Brookings Institution, 2006).
11. The link between condos and affluence is clear. The number of condominiums increased by an average of 124 percent in the 21 cities in which relative per capita income increased between 2000 and 2007.
12. Allison Klein, "Major Cities' Plummeting Crime Rates Mystifying," *Washington Post*, July 20, 2009.
13. Heron Marquez Estrada and Anthony Lonetree, "Drop in Crime Is a Victory," Minneapolis *StarTribune*, July 24, 2009.
14. William H. Frey, *Big City Populations Survive the Housing Crunch* (Washington, D.C.: Brookings Institution, 2009).
15. Hope Yen, "Big Cities See Resurgence in Population Growth," Associated Press, July 1, 2009.
16. Eric Pryne, "Will Steep Price Cuts Fill High-End Condos?" *Seattle Times*, July 14, 2009.
17. James Temple, "Recession a Blow to Revitalization," *San Francisco Chronicle*, July 12, 2009.
18. Michelle E. Shaw, "Economy Derails Mixed-use Projects," *Atlanta Journal-Constitution*, August 2, 2009.
19. Christine Armario, "Fla. Highrise Has 32 Stories, but Just 1 Tenant," Associated Press, August 2, 2009.

3

Old Neighborhoods Lead the Way

For the past 15 to 20 years, my wife, Sherry, has been remarking, as we drive through some part of Albemarle County—outside Charlottesville, Virginia, where we live—that she would love to live out there. We would be several miles away from town, in a rural area with a view of the Blue Ridge Mountains. She could enjoy going home each day to the restful beauty of the rural countryside: a glorious view of farms, hills, and mountains.

The lure for her would be a sense of retreat. For people with active, often stressful days of meeting, negotiating, serving, and managing other people of any age, a period of after-work repose must seem inviting. For others, the lure is sheer space. I know of two retirees who moved to the Charlottesville area from an inner-ring suburb and chose an exurban house on a wooded lot of two or three acres, too large for two people but with room for children and grandchildren and a large sculpture studio. Others seek a safer place to raise children, or enough open land to let dogs run free, or a brand-new house they can shape for themselves.

We have never made that move.

In the end, Sherry and I both prefer the conveniences of our own neighborhood, known as North Downtown. We can walk three blocks to downtown and find an eight-block-long pedestrian mall, shaded by 62 trees, most of them 60-foot-high willow oaks, with only two vehicle crossings. The mall is a gathering place for rich and poor, including numerous homeless people, young and old, and everyone in between. Every once in a while I hear of someone who's afraid to go there; but it can't be a very common sentiment, because on two recent Friday nights I counted 660 and 707 outdoor diners on the mall at 8:30 p.m. Between 6:00 and 11:00 p.m., tables can turn over three and four times in a single evening.

If both places hold some attraction for both of us, however, the more walkable of the two gets more and more appealing the older we get. The more we age, the less interested we are in a form of living in which, as the conservative humorist P. J. O'Rourke observed,

> Americans had to spend all of their time driving. The play date was 40 miles from the Chuck E. Cheese. The swim meet was 40 miles from the cello lesson. The Montessori was 40 miles from the math coach. Mom's job was 40 miles from Dad's job and the three-car garage was 40 miles from both.[1]

Suburbs and exurbs became such a dominant theme in our culture over the last half of the 20th century because they suited the preferences of Americans at the time.

In 1950, 50 percent of households were families with children under 18. The suburban dream typically includes residence in single-unit detached houses, daily use of automobiles, commuting to workplaces where free parking is provided, location within a small jurisdiction where public school and land-use policies can be influenced by residents, and no obvious evidence of poverty nearby. The federal government created a secondary mortgage market to expand home ownership and built 42,000 miles of interstate highways that allowed people to live far away from their jobs.

Suburbs sought to keep the poor out, and their zoning encouraged work sites with free parking. Poverty remained in older areas, out of sight for residents of newer suburbs.

And most of this can be traced back to who we were as a people: our demographics. A large majority of households had children at home, previously had children at home, or anticipated having children at home. Along with demographics came the price of energy: Gas was cheap, allowing us to buy lots of large vehicles. Energy was cheap for heating and cooling large homes.

Today, these twin platforms for the suburban dream have eroded. They haven't vanished, but they are weakening. We aren't the same people, and energy prices are higher.

Fewer than one-third of households have children at home. Even fewer such households are expected in the future. Less than 50 percent of households, in other words, buy homes based on where parents want their *children* to live—a huge issue for the past 60 years.

The folks in today's America who correspond to those 1950s *Leave It To Beaver* families are just as likely to be minorities. Although people of color still make up only 34 percent of our population, they already account for almost half the babies born each year and are close to outnumbering whites in that department.[2] Already, in just over 500 counties (about one in six), minorities outnumber whites among those people younger than 20.

The perceptions of safety, of better schools, of nicer parks are drawing minorities out to the suburbs for the same reasons they drew whites. At the same time, the prototypical white baby boomer family consists of parents in their fifties with empty nests (or nearing that point), and their children are nearing (or in) young adulthood, one of the periods in our lives when city life appeals to us the most.

This is the most basic explanation for the frenzy of condominium building in the past 10 years or so. The Urban Land Institute, an organization of large developers, has been making the case for several years that development opportunities

increasingly will be in new developments created within existing cities, near train and bus stops.[3]

No one was coordinating all the decisions to build these
condos or capping the number of units at what the market
would support, so they were overbuilt. And the existence of
large numbers of empty units is one thing that has raised questions in peoples' minds about the true strength of the urban
population comeback. But the developers were not mistaken
about the basic direction in which we're heading.

The period from roughly age 25 to 45 is when living at home,
or renting a place, changes into home ownership. When we are
25 to 29, only 40.6 percent of us own homes.[4] That jumps to
54.4 percent when we're 30 to 34, and to 67.8 percent as we
reach the ages of 35 to 44. When we're older still, these numbers rise further: to between 75.4 and 80.6 percent. But increasingly these folks are no longer in their young-family homes.

It stands to reason, then, that demand for housing declined
in some suburban parts of metropolitan areas, usually outer
areas, due to shifts in the age distribution of the population.
The population segment from age 30 to 44, when the biggest
increase in home ownership occurs, started declining in 2004.
In 2008, there were 1.7 million fewer households headed by
someone age 30 to 44 than in 2003. Those are prime child-
rearing years for families, so demand for houses with four or
more bedrooms declined and led to an excess of large houses
in some counties.[5]

In fact, the demographic shifts are so profound that there
may soon be a huge excess of large suburban homes. Based
on condominium and single-family detached housing price
trends, market surveys of consumer preferences, and the aging
of the population, planning scholar Arthur Nelson concluded
that "market demand for new homes through 2025 may be
almost exclusively for attached and small-lot units." Others
have warned more ominously that the post-2000 housing bubble may be followed by a 20-year age-based excess of houses
in suburbs, starting soon after 2010 in some states, caused by
the presence of more sellers age 65 and over than there are
replacement buyers.[6] An aging stock of housing was almost

certainly another factor in the declines we've seen in suburban incomes.

True, some aging suburbs manage to hold on and remain stable despite the cancer of decline all around them. Alexandria, Virginia, has grown in population and thrived in income and economic activity despite—or perhaps because of—its age. Oak Park, Illinois, adjacent to Chicago, is another case in point. But this has to do with the places themselves: people who know the Washington or Chicago areas well, who have seen Alexandria or Oak Park, will have no problem understanding why they do well.

Generally speaking, though, the age of housing in both cities and suburbs forecasts how they will do. In the 1990s, the most recent stretch of time we can examine in a fine-grained way at this point, old neighborhoods did better than those built in any decade except the newest ones, those built mainly in the 1990s. There seemed to be a quest for the newly built and the older full of character, and a flight away from those in the middle.

This was a change from the way things had gone in the past.

When we examined 8,471 census tracts in the cities and suburbs of six metropolitan areas (Atlanta, Chicago, Los Angeles, Philadelphia, Richmond, and Washington, D.C.), we found that, in the 1990s, the conventional pattern of housing and neighborhood decline (as housing ages, it is passed down from middle-income and upper-income households to moderate- and low-income households) changed.

By 2000, pre-1940 census tracts no longer were the lowest-income areas within their metros. Tracts dominated by housing whose origins overlapped the 1940s and 1950s were occupied by families with lower incomes than neighborhoods specializing in pre-1940s housing. Middle-aged census tracts, those developed from 1950 to 1970, were most likely to have fallen, or to be falling, to lower income levels relative to metropolitan averages (Table 3.1).

How to explain this? Why were middle-aged areas falling while older ones were rising? To really nail that down will take further research. But we are guessing that the causes were house sizes and neighborhood settings.

TABLE 3.1 RELATIVE AVERAGE FAMILY INCOME INCREASES FOR TRACTS HIGHLY SPECIALIZED IN HOUSING CONSTRUCTED IN DIFFERENT DECADES

CONSTRUCTION	CHANGE 1980 TO 1990			CHANGE 1990 TO 2000		
	All Tracts	Central City	Outside City	All Tracts	Central City	Outside City
Pre-1940						
Tracts	1076	774	302	1101	776	325
Increased	349	221	128	547	387	160
Percent Increased	32.4	28.6	42.4	49.7	49.9	49.2
1940s						
Tracts	751	404	347	759	404	355
Increased	166	85	81	298	149	149
Percent Increased	22.1	21.0	23.3	39.3	36.9	42.0
1950s						
Tracts	626	175	451	629	174	455
Increased	93	30	63	177	43	134
Percent Increased	14.9	17.1	14.0	28.1	24.7	29.5
1960s						
Tracts	417	81	336	417	81	336
Increased	83	16	67	86	19	67
Percent Increased	19.9	19.8	19.9	20.6	23.5	19.9
1970s						
Tracts	434	32	402	435	32	403
Increased	165	8	157	120	10	110
Percent Increased	38.0	25.0	39.1	27.6	31.3	27.3
1980s						
Tracts	44	44	702	750	46	704
Increased	359	20	339	305	16	289
Percent Increased	48.1	45.5	48.3	40.7	34.8	41.1

TABLE 3.1 (CONTINUED)

CONSTRUCTION	CHANGE 1980 TO 1990			CHANGE 1990 TO 2000		
	All Tracts	Central City	Outside City	All Tracts	Central City	Outside City
Since 1980						
Tracts				790	38	752
Increased				449	23	426
Percent Increased				56.8	60.5	56.6

In this table a tract is considered "highly specialized" if it has 2.5 times or more of the metropolitan proportion of housing built in that decade. This table uses data reported in the 2000 Census of Population and Housing. The proportion of a census tract's occupied housing in a particular period of construction is compared with the proportion for its metropolitan area. These census tracts were in the metropolitan areas of Atlanta, Chicago, Los Angeles, Philadelphia, Richmond, and Washington, D.C.

If a census tract's average family income relative to its metropolitan area's average family income grew by more than 2.5%, it is reported here as "Increased."

Source: Neighborhood Change Database (NCDB) Tract Data from 1970–2000 and CensusCD 2000, Geolytics (East Brunswick, N.J., 2003). This table appeared in William H. Lucy and David L. Phillips, *Tomorrow's Cities, Tomorrow's Suburbs* (Chicago: APA Planners Press, 2006).

In 1950 the median size of a new house (half bigger, half smaller) was 1,100 square feet. That rose to 1,375 by 1970. By 2005, it was 2,235 square feet, doubling from 1950 and up 60 percent since 1970.

Homes also got fancier throughout that time. By the end, no longer was there just one bath, no central air-conditioning, or only two or three small bedrooms.

Between 1945 and 1970, Americans also separated land uses. Homes began to be removed from areas of stores, offices, and industry. No one wanted to live next to a gas station, with bright lights on well into the night. Neighborhoods were configured in such a way as to reduce traffic: cul-de-sacs appeared, turning city streets into little more than private drives for a handful of folks.

Many suburbs were developed almost entirely during the 25 years following World War II. They are most likely to be dominated by small houses, far from shops and other needs. While some continue to be success stories (Levittown, on Long Island, in New York, is an example), many more have declined.

Pre-1940 neighborhoods (certainly not all of them, but many) were widely varied in their housing types and quality, nearly always were more accessible, sometimes were in prime areas, including close to downtown jobs, and became attractive places to remodel or to demolish and rebuild. In city after city and in some inner suburbs, "monster home" became a term of abuse, as families wanting these close-in locations but more space wiped out homes that had been in scale with their surroundings and built taller, fatter ones instead.

There were other problems with many bedroom suburbs from the post–World War II era. Few had strong, or really any, downtowns. Instead, they had shopping centers. These succeeded for many years, but many declined into pawn shops and thrift stores en route to being vacant. Some have been demolished.

Small-house suburbs, coupled with faded or failed shopping centers, are not prime generators of land values or property tax revenues. And their prospects, in general, are not good, though some are in locations that have become attractive. For instance, some have become stations for light-rail lines or are fairly close to an airport.

At the same time, cities have a lot more going for them than the grim descriptions of them circa 1990 would imply. Many have been making comebacks, especially in their downtowns, because they retained major assets.

Cities had big sources of money. They got federal and state aid, and they retained the loyalty of many members of the region's economic elites, rich enough to contribute and invest.

Even if they lost shoppers to suburban malls, they still were places to which many went to work in offices, in finance, in government. Lawyers still wanted to walk to state and federal courts. Hotels, restaurants, convention centers, museums, and performance venues were there, in fact increasingly so as cities fought back against suburban challenges by installing more and more of them. Some of these activities appealed to young households and empty-nesters. These assets have been driving reinvestment in many cities.

Most small suburbs lack these assets. Their once-solid residential neighborhoods often have deteriorated. In the process, many neighborhoods have lost one of their main attractions: dependability and predictability.

In theory, of course, buyers could come in and improve those small homes. But when neighborhoods are dominated by small houses, with little variation in age, size, and quality, buyers have to pause and think. Renovating a house is annoying, time consuming, and expensive. Finding a reliable, affordable builder is challenging. Mastering zoning regulations takes time. Borrowing the money, if home equity is insufficient, may be difficult. Financing two residences, in some instances, during construction may not be affordable.

And then, how does one know what direction the neighborhood is heading? Will others like me come next, or will they pass on this street, so that I find myself living beside poor families with junk cars in a seedy front yard, and my investment evaporates? Similar risks confront developers. Developers nearly always find easier, less risky, and more profitable alternatives.

Places like this don't do well at retaining and attracting young, well-educated professionals with children who are seeking larger, better equipped houses, or empty-nesters who may want smaller places but who don't want to have to drive to everything and seldom want the stresses of remodeling and expanding.

The exurbs, meanwhile, have a differing problem: gas price volatility. During the 1990s and early 2000s, as house prices rose, developers talked of buyers who "drove to affordability": opted for homes much farther away from things than they ever imagined, but as far away as they needed to be in order to be able to afford a larger home. In one metro area after another, communities that had always been thought of as "rural," far from commuting belts, began sprouting lookalike beige subdivisions.

The average person in those days, however, could not have imagined an America in which people paid four dollars per gallon for gas. Those prices didn't last long; but the memory of shocking volatility remains.

High foreclosure rates in many outer suburbs by 2008 suggested that a combination of circumstances reduced demand, preventing many home owners from solving their inability to pay their mortgages by selling and breaking even or making a profit. Their house values had sunk below their mortgage amount, rendering them "under water" and unable to sell without losing money in the sale.

The weaknesses of suburbs and exurbs should lead to greater financial strength in cities. If public services improve in cities, these also will provide an attraction. A more affluent population will lead to less crime in cities and perhaps more crime in suburbs. If city public schools improve, the trickle of middle-income families with children back to cities may become a substantial stream.

One sign of this potential came in 2009 in New York City's Lower Manhattan. Hundreds of parents protested the proposed elimination of prekindergarten education and waiting lists for kindergarteners. They criticized Mayor Michael Bloomberg and School Chancellor Joel Klein for encouraging residential development but not adding enough school spaces. The explanation: The mayor and school chancellor may reasonably have expected condominiums to fill up with empty-nesters, retirees, and young single professionals. Instead, many young families with children of school age bought condos close to work, entertainment, and shopping—and close also, they thought, to schools.[7]

In addition, job trends may support city revival. Job loss in central cities is a frequent lament of urban analysts and public officials. But this claim often is overstated or even mistaken. Most cities contained more jobs than residents of employable ages looking for work in 2000. Detroit was one of the few exceptions.

Between 1998 and 2001, 33 of 36 large cities in our sample actually increased employment. Detroit, St. Louis, and Buffalo were the exceptions. The average increase was 4.9 percent, a percentage exceeded in 16 cities. In 15 of these 16 cities, relative per capita incomes of non-Hispanic whites were higher in the cities than in the metropolitan area overall. Why? Probably because highly educated workers, who were white more often than not, were mainly employed in the "new economy" jobs (professions, education, health, government, finance, insurance, and information) that were the source of job growth in cities. Thus, the connection between work and residential locations that the suburban era had cast aside was still evident in the 1990s and after 2000, if only slightly (Table 3.2).

Each of these trends supports other trends favoring central city revival. Just as central cities faced a cascade of mutually reinforcing reasons for decline in the 1960s and 1970s, more recent trends are going in the opposite direction and are likely to be accompanied by a cascade of reasons for more rapid decline in many suburbs.

The data suggest, in short, that there is every reason to expect the following in the future:

- As the percentage of households with children declines, and that of singles, empty-nesters, and elderly increases, housing demand will increase in cities and inner suburbs, and demand in outer suburbs and exurbs will level off or decline nationally, with considerable variation among metropolitan areas and regions of the nation.
- Suburban decline will accelerate in middle-aged housing, but that won't be uniform: demand for housing in some inner suburbs will rise.
- Many low-income households, especially minorities, will relocate, pushed by higher housing costs in areas with transportation alternatives, often to less dense and less convenient neighborhoods farther from the center of cities and inner suburbs.
- In metropolitan areas where demand for large houses on large lots falls, housing-price deflation in outer counties will occur, and doubling and tripling up of low- and moderate-income households in large houses will become common.
- Demand will increase for transit serving more areas more frequently.
- Demand for more mixed use and walkable neighborhoods will increase, and prices in these areas will escalate as supply lags behind demand.

TABLE 3.2 EMPLOYMENT CHARACTERISTICS OF PRINCIPAL CITIES

PRINCIPAL CITY	EMPLOYMENT IN CITY RELATIVE TO CITY POPULATION[2]	EMPLOYMENT CHANGE 1998 TO 2001[1]	
		PRINCIPAL CITY	METROPOLITAN AREA
Atlanta	98.1	9.6	11.0
Baltimore	47.3	2.2	6.8
Boston	64.0	7.5	6.4
Buffalo	49.9	-0.9	1.9
Charlotte	75.9	12.4	10.4
Chicago	43.1	4.1	4.5
Cincinnati	81.8	1.6	3.7
Cleveland	61.2	1.1	3.2
Columbus	57.6	1.8	6.4
Dallas	64.4	1.5	8.7
Denver	74.8	8.9	10.2
Detroit	27.1	-2.5	1.3
Houston	65.4	4.7	5.9
Indianapolis	78.4	5.4	6.2
Kansas City	54.4	6.5	7.4
Las Vegas	43.0	13.0	15.4
Los Angeles	34.2	4.8	5.0
Miami	60.7	3.5	1.2
Milwaukee	47.4	0.5	1.6
Minneapolis	44.9	2.1	6.3
New York	41.3	7.5	7.5
Newport News			
Norfolk		0.7	4.7

TABLE 3.2 (CONTINUED)

PRINCIPAL CITY	EMPLOYMENT IN CITY RELATIVE TO CITY POPULATION[2]	EMPLOYMENT CHANGE 1998 TO 2001[1]	
		PRINCIPAL CITY	METROPOLITAN AREA
Oakland		6.4	11.3
Orlando	112.0	16.0	8.8
Philadelphia	40.6	3.8	5.6
Phoenix	39.6	6.1	9.2
Pittsburgh	96.8	3.2	3.1
Portland	67.3	1.1	4.8
Sacramento	46.0	10.1	13.8
San Antonio	44.6	8.5	9.8
San Diego	50.3	9.4	11.2
San Francisco	71.8	4.7	8.2
Seattle	75.5	5.4	8.2
St. Louis	78.8	-1.3	2.2
St. Paul			
St. Petersburg			
Tampa	51.2	0.9	6.3
Virginia Beach			
Washington, D.C.	55.3	4.8	6.9
Averages	60.2	4.9	6.8

[1] Edward W. Hill and John Brennan, "America's Central Cities and the Location of Work," *Journal of the American Planning Association* 71, no. 4 (2005): 429–32.

[2] Calculated from employment and population data in ibid., 411–32.

One final thought. The average person probably vaguely thinks that we have to keep sprawling ever outward, because after all, our inner areas are already settled, already developed, already built on. Where would we put people, if not to pave over the next cornfield out from the outermost rim of suburbia?

The truth, though, if we choose for it to happen, is that a tremendously high proportion of our future growth as a nation could easily occur within already developed areas: in, or on the edges of, big-city downtowns; on busy corners of city streets away from downtown; and in new urban villages close to high-speed transit stations in suburbs.

The zones of opportunity for new formats, new and more compact neighborhoods, take several forms.

EMPTY DOWNTOWN BLOCKS

Aerial photos of our downtowns can render visible a fact that we all sort of understand but seldom stop to think about: they are full of blank spots—ragged, weedy spots of dirt and parking lots that could be moved underground. That's one big reason why it's possible to report the remarkable fact that "from 2001 through 2008, more than 8,000 condominium units were built in downtown San Diego."[8] And it's one reason why it can be said that even in a city as tightly built already as Portland, Oregon, "there are 15,000 acres of vacant, buildable land within the current urban growth boundary . . . about 35 times the size of downtown Portland."[9]

BLANK SPOTS ON THE MAP

A flyover of many cities would also reveal that there are a number of large-acreage spaces that would be attractive to condo buyers for various reasons—often because they're on waterfronts—but either aren't being used at all or are being put to uses that could readily be moved elsewhere. On closer inspection, some of these areas will prove to have ground contamination too costly for private developers to remove. But many other areas that from the air seem to have substantial structures on them are revealed on the ground to be occupied by one-story buildings that are unoccupied or underutilized and beg for more intensive redevelopment.

In the Atlanta area, for instance, planners in Cobb County are eyeing an industrial area:

> The county's proposed River Line plan states that the industrial nature of south Cobb's riverfront will gradually fade over the next decade, to be replaced by walking trails, townhomes, houses and a cute community retail center like Vinings Jubilee.
>
> Developer Green Street Properties, which built the Glenwood Park community near Grant Park, has bought 86 acres in the last three years, smack in the middle of the industrial area near the Chattahoochee. The company may seek a rezoning to build a walkable development of homes, retail and office space, company Vice President Amy Swick said.[10]

In the Seattle area, the same is true of Point Wells, "61 acres of west-facing waterfront," now bearing an asphalt plant and oil-tank farm but which could house 6,000 new residents in buildings as high as 16 stories.[11] In the San Francisco Bay area, 30,000 people could move into a waterfront zone that since 1901 "has been used as industrial salt evaporation ponds to produce salt for roads, food and medicine . . . environmentalists say that because the property was once part of the bay's teeming marshes and sloughs, all of it should be restored to habitat for fish, birds and other wildlife."

> The project, which DMB will submit to the city Tuesday, includes a mixture of condominiums, apartments and attached housing on half the 1,433-acre site. There also would be 1 million square feet of office space, retail shops, a fire station, and a trolley system that would connect residents with downtown Redwood City and its Caltrain station, slightly less than a mile away across Highway 101.[12]

OTHER COMMON SETTINGS

Just outside many of our downtowns are inner city ghettos full of decaying homes and empty lots, and there are proposals in many places to seize that land and do something with it. In St. Louis, a developer is proposing an $8 billion plan to revitalize 1,500 acres of the city across the river from downtown to the north.[13] In Los Angeles, the city is considering a $1 billion makeover of Watts.[14] In Cincinnati, the idea comes coupled with a streetcar line:

The proposed route and surrounding blocks now are dotted by 92 acres of surface parking and dozens of abandoned or under-used buildings that city leaders and consultants consider ripe for redevelopment.[15]

And even in parts of town that are not as desolate, cities have the option of locating many more people in parts of town that are already fully built out but often only lightly settled.

Since 2006, more than 1,700 residential units have been built in and around [Cambridge's] Kendall Square.[16]

What would San Jose look like if gleaming high-rises suddenly sprouted all across the city? A proposal that would place three 15-story towers . . . just west of downtown . . . has added to the debate about the future character of a city that's traditionally embraced tract housing.[17]

Like many neighborhoods inside Loop 610, Cottage Grove in recent years has experienced a flurry of construction of large townhomes that loom over 80-year-old cottages next door.[18]

A glance at the headlines of the articles in which these statements appear, however, will show that anything of this sort always draws tremendous opposition from political left and right alike. It sometimes seems as though the one thing industry and environmentalists, conservative suburbanites and liberal city-dwellers, rich and poor can all agree on is that they don't want dense new development nearby.

And that leads us to the next important point. As a society, we are in some suspense at this moment about where the next big development push will or should take place: on the edge or in the center. There are attractions to both. But what, in fact, *should* be happening next?

NOTES

1. P. J. O'Rourke, "The End of the Affair," *Wall Street Journal*, May 30, 2009.
2. The percentage of minority births in 2008 was 48. Haya El Nasser, "Minority Kids Grow to a Majority," *USA Today*, June 17, 2009, 1A.

3. PriceWaterhouseCoopers, *Emerging Trends in Real Estate* (Washington, D.C.: Urban Land Institute, 2006).

4. Based upon data from 2007. U.S. Department of Housing and Urban Development, *U.S. Housing Market Conditions: Historical Data* (2008), Table 27.

5. See Appendix 1 for more details on this point.

6. Changes in age cohorts may reduce demand for the housing types that the baby boom generation, now moving toward retirement, preferred for the child-rearing years. See Dowell Myers and SungHo Ryu, "Aging Baby Boomers and the Generational Housing Bubble," *Journal of the American Planning Association* 74 (winter 2008): 17–33.

7. Albert Amateau, "Overcrowding Outrage Erupts; Hundreds Decry Lack of Seats," The *Villager*, May 13–19, 2009.

8. Peter Y. Hong, "Condo Frenzy Turns to Fizzle," *Los Angeles Times*, July 27, 2009, 1A.

9. Eric Mortenson, "New to Town? Squeeze In," Portland *Oregonian*, September 16, 2009, 1A.

10. Mary Jo Pickel, "Industry Fears Riverfront Plan," *Atlanta Journal-Constitution*, August 25, 2009, 1A.

11. Lynn Thompson, "Proposed Massive Development Worries Point Wells Neighbors," *Seattle Times*, July 27, 2009, 1A.

12. Paul Rogers, "'Smart Growth' along S.F. Bay?" *San Jose Mercury News*, May 13, 2009, 1A.

13. Tim Logan, "Big Splash or Block by Block?" *St. Louis Post-Dispatch*, June 29, 2009, 1A.

14. Ari B. Bloomekatz and Jessica Garrison, "L.A. Plans $1-billion Face-lift in Watts: The City Aims to Turn Notorious Gang Turf into an Urban Village," *Los Angeles Times*, February 28, 2009, 1A.

15. Barry M. Horstman, "Streetcar Backers Have Backs to Wall," Cincinnati *Enquirer*, May 14, 2009, 1A.

16. Jenifer B. McKim, "Kendall Starting to Work as a Home," *Boston Globe*, September 16, 2009, 1A.

17. Denis C. Theriault, "Are Towers a Glimpse of Future?" *San Jose Mercury News*, August 25, 2009, 1A.

18. Mike Snyder, "How Urban Can Houston Become? As Density Sprawls from Loop to Beltway, Big Changes to Our Development Code Loom. But Some Worry Flooding, Parking and Other Problems Will Follow," *Houston Chronicle*, June 29, 2009, 1A.

4

Coping with Global Warming

Despite the many signs of an urban turnaround—of a turning away from sprawl and a renewed interest in the health and attractions of the centers of our metro areas—it remains to be seen precisely what will happen at the center and the edge. Sprawl satisfies the needs of many powerful people, including business interests and city and county officials at the edge. Both groups have bet a tremendous amount of money on growth, and both will suffer in various ways if growth ceases. Both the fancy new sports bar and the $5 million water-treatment plant were financed on the belief that new customers, new home buyers, and new tax base would continue to flow in.

So it's not just a matter of pointing to the trends and retiring from the scene. There is also the importance of insuring the continuation of this turnaround, for the sake of the planet: to reduce pollution, to cut down on greenhouse gases, and to save on the use of nonrenewable oil.

TRANSPORTATION AND OIL

Before one can figure out what to do, one needs to know the facts about energy.

In 2005, this is where energy went:

- 21.5 percent to homes
- 17.8 percent to stores and other commercial buildings
- 32.5 percent to factories
- 28.1 percent to cars and other forms of transportation[1]

Transportation produced 28 percent of greenhouse gas emissions in the United States in 2004.[2] Just over half of petroleum products are used for transportation (44 percent for motor vehicles, 8 percent for planes). Within the car and truck sector, 43 percent of fuel consumption is in passenger cars and motorcycles, 38 percent in SUVs and pick-up trucks, and 19 percent in freight trucks. Most of the remainder is used for heating oil and propane.[3]

Transportation is the part of the energy picture most dependent on policies of federal, state, and local government officials. If they can reorder the way people get around—through new rail transit, for instance—and combine that with new development patterns, they can improve the quality of metropolitan life.

Transportation also directly affects military preparedness, foreign policy, the cost of living, inflation, and—because of oil imports—the balance of payments in international trade.

Crude oil imports increased by 304 percent between 1970 and 2005.[4] During that period, consumption of petroleum products increased by 41.5 percent,[5] and U.S. oil production dropped by 46 percent. By 2007, the United States imported 66 percent of its oil.[6]

The amount of petroleum consumed affects climate change and resource depletion, but importing oil adds many additional effects: economic, military, diplomatic, and political.

REDUCING ENERGY USE IN TRANSPORTATION

Because energy consumption in transportation is high in the United States, reducing it should be easy. Average mileage in motor vehicles in household use in the United States in 2005 was about 22 miles per gallon (mpg) for cars and 17 for light trucks,[7] compared with 43 mpg for cars in Europe and 46 in Japan.[8] These differences are partly a result of vehicle efficiency, but they have been influenced more by consumers' choices of which vehicles to use. Americans could all use a lot less oil if they bought different vehicles.

Truckers may have a harder time with that. But they can reduce speeds and thus increase mileage—and many did just that during the run-up in diesel prices in 2007 and 2008.

Shippers could use more rail, which consumes less fuel than trucks. And they are: rail freight increased from 29 billion car miles in 1980 to 36 billion in 2003. But tractor-trailer truck transport increased more: from 69 million miles in 1980 to 139 million in 2002. Air cargo grew even more, from five billion ton miles in 1980 to almost 17 billion in 2004.[9] In short, freight modes that consumed more energy increased the most.

Government isn't exactly helping. The contrast between government spending in the United States and Europe is striking. European nations invested 26 billion euros in rail transportation facilities in 2001, compared with just $737 million by the United States.[10] Rail plays a key role in Europe. In 2005, the Trans-European Transport Network added 16 projects and corridors to the 14 that then carried more than half of all European freight and passenger traffic.[11]

TECHNOFIX?

Presidents and presidential candidates on both sides—George W. Bush, Al Gore, John Kerry, Barack Obama, Hillary Clinton, John McCain—have emphasized the transformative potential of renewable energy technologies. It's a lot more attractive to hope for a technofix than to ask Americans to make real changes in their lives. And in fact, much can be accomplished along these lines. But it's very unlikely to happen as quickly as needed in order to avoid risking disaster.

After analyzing potential gains from the federal Energy Independence and Security Act of 2007, one team of researchers concluded:

> Optimistically assuming that fuel economy for new passenger vehicles could rise as high as 45 mpg by 2030 and that the carbon content of fuels could be reduced by 15 percent, CO_2

emissions from cars and light trucks would remain 8 percent above 1990 levels.[12]

The challenge of reducing CO_2 emissions from transportation is apparent in trend lines revealed in the National Household Travel Survey of 2001 and its periodic predecessor surveys since 1969. From 1969 to 2001, partly because Americans grew more and more dispersed across the landscape, the number of households increased 72 percent, the number of vehicles 181 percent, the number of vehicle trips 169 percent, and the number of vehicle miles 194 percent.[13]

GOALS FOR HOUSEHOLDS AND GOVERNMENTS

We all could be doing more. A plausible goal for households could be to make at least 50 percent of daily trips by means other than driving alone. We could use public transportation, bike, walk, or carpool. To put this in context, such a change would put us in the same general ballpark as Europeans.

What would that mean? With average trips per household at about 10 per day (five leaving, five coming back), four trips per day per household by means other than driving alone in motor vehicles would be needed to achieve 50 percent of trips by modes other than driving alone.[14] But that's not realistic for those who live in subdivisions five miles from the nearest convenience store and 20 miles from the nearest Target or Best Buy. We can't change that much unless we're located nearer the places we need to go.

In 2005, 77 percent of trips by commuters were made alone in motor vehicles. (Just under 11 percent were made by carpooling.)[15] That makes the goal of half of all trips made by means other than driving alone seem implausible.

But consider: in New York City, with many people tucked into very little space and effective public transportation, only 25 percent of commuter trips were driven alone in 2000. And it's not just big cities. In Charlottesville, Virginia, for example, 25 percent of residents in the neighborhood just north of downtown walked to work in 2000. So did 40 percent of those living near the University of Virginia.[16] Living close to work always has a lot to do with vehicle miles traveled. If people live in areas close to jobs and shops, they walk a lot more. For trips other than work, 32 percent walked in the Metro Square area of Sacramento, compared with a regional average of 7 percent.[17]

In parts of some metropolitan areas, mainly central cities, people already achieve the household goals we've mentioned. But not overall—not even in New York. Densities outside central cities are too low for many households to achieve these goals. Sprawl is the main reason for average annual distance traveled per motor vehicle increasing 30 percent from 1970 to 2000.[18]

Any commuter who can reach a train, subway, light-rail stop, streetcar, or bus by walking or biking can achieve the goal of 50 percent or fewer trips by driving alone. Every metropolitan area has some places where those who wish to do this can.

The challenge is that most metropolitan areas are not organized with land development and transportation options that make achieving these goals possible for most residents. Making that happen will be difficult.

CROSS-NATIONAL COMPARISONS

By 2006, Europe reduced its greenhouse gas emissions more than 7 percent below 1990 levels, mainly by reducing emissions from residential and commercial buildings.[19] Although Europe has not reduced transportation emissions in recent years, it remains far below the United States in personal motor vehicle use and greenhouse gas emissions from transportation.

As ambitious as they sound for us, the goals we've discussed are simply realities in other industrial and postindustrial nations. In 2004, kilometers traveled in motor vehicles per capita were:[20]

United States	23,095
Canada	15,169
France	12,977
Sweden	11,619
United Kingdom	11,614
Germany	10,186
Japan	6,602

There are four signs that substantial movement toward European patterns is possible.

First, Europe has demonstrated how these goals can be achieved, and as a result Europeans paid less for transportation.[21] While transportation accounted for 18 percent of household expenditures in the U.S. Consumer Price Index for December 2007,[22] the same figure was 12 percent in Europe.[23]

Second, as we've seen, some trends have moved Americans closer to European patterns since 1990.

Third, it is increasingly recognized that prices for fuel and vulnerabilities of petroleum supplies from nations that are volatile or hostile to the United States make change prudent.

And fourth, Europe arguably has achieved a higher quality of life in its metropolitan areas than exists for most people in U.S. metropolitan areas.[24]

Critics of compact development sometimes claim transportation behavior and land use patterns in Europe have become more like those in the United States.[25] That claim is exaggerated. European nations have been coping with a modest increase in sprawl and a modest dip in transit use, but they are still leagues apart from us.[26] The size of the difference between the United States and Europe indicates the large reduction in energy consumption and greenhouse gas emissions that the United States eventually can achieve through transportation and land use changes.

POLITICAL SUPPORT FOR TRANSIT

The trends taking place today should increase support for transit investments: more affluent and powerful people are moving to cities and older suburbs. But the politics of achieving national majorities in Congress for transit investments will remain difficult. Given where most people live, they will emphasize less congested highway travel, not transit access. Many states lack metropolitan areas with sufficient density to make transit cost effective any time soon. That reality creates counterpressures in Congress against a major transition toward transit and away from highways.

The politics of actually making transit work on the ground also are difficult. Rationally speaking, Americans shouldn't be spending a lot of money to create, say, a high-speed bus line, unless there's long-term financing for networks of lines, coupled with a determination to enable lots of transit users to live close to stations. But a congressional majority is created through spreading transit spending across most states and congressional districts. There are pressures to reduce the focus on density and increase pork-barrel allocations to districts representing a working majority of votes in Congress.

These national political difficulties lead to the necessity of action by states. State elected officials may see more clearly the importance of both transit investments and more density where transit is installed.

POLICIES TO INCREASE TRANSIT USE

Federal transportation policies are still dominated by decisions made in the 1950s to build and finance the 46,876-mile system of interstate highways. The federal gasoline tax is still targeted overwhelmingly for highways. Despite that, gas-tax revenues were not enough to finance federal highway maintenance, reconstruction, and construction. It took special $6 billion Congressional allocations in 2008 and 2009 to close that gap.

States went along with federal plans for the interstate highway system because the federal share was 90 percent of the construction costs from their own highway trust fund. Developers and home owners seized opportunities provided by the interstate system to live farther out. Sprawl contributed to increased carbon emissions. From 1980 to 2005, carbon emissions from transportation and buildings increased more than 25 percent.

Consumers became, and remain, the driving force in energy consumption and carbon emissions. Industrial emissions diminished during this period as manufacturing declined and knowledge-based industries expanded.[27] Federal tax policies inevitably encourage more use of some energy types and less use of other types. Future tax policies will need to support renewable sources and penalize nonrenewable sources.

Transit got more and more attention in major transportation funding bills in 1991, 1998, and 2005. But by 2008 the federal government still contributed 80 to 90 percent of the cost of major highway projects and only 50 to 60 percent of major transit projects. Many proposed transit projects were rejected because of insufficient federal funds. The willingness to subsidize highways more suggests a national bias. Instead, as Robert Puentes argues, "the federal government should . . . pursue a strategy of 'modality neutrality.' Transportation policy should enable metro areas to meet their goals on economy, competitiveness, environment sustainability, and/or equity by the best means available, rather than being constrained by rules governing a particular mode."[28]

Metropolitan areas acting through metropolitan planning organizations (MPOs) should develop integrated transportation, land use, economic development, and housing plans. Federal funds should contribute to achieving these plans by whichever transportation modes are most effective.

Transit spending as a share of total transportation spending has been stable (21 percent in 1985, 19 percent in 1990, 20 percent in 1995, and 18 percent in 2001). The share of total transportation spending on highways also was unchanged from 1985 (60.4 percent) to 2001 (60.3 percent).[29] By 2000, the landmark federal transportation bill of 1991 had not led to substantial changes in the federal, state, and local shares of capital spending for transit.[30]

A national study for the American Association of State Highway and Transportation Officials estimated $45.3 billion in capital investments is needed annually to upgrade public transportation, whereas actual capital spending has been only $12.5 billion.[31] About $50 billion in capital reinvestment is needed just to maintain safe operation of the seven largest U.S. transit systems.[32] To achieve European levels of transit use, far more transit investment would be required.

Even as federal support for transit has been limited, state and local support has risen. There is an

> increasing willingness of voters to raise taxes for a variety of transit, open space, and related smart growth initiatives . . . passing

more than three-quarters of them from 1994 to 2006, generating more than \$110 billion in revenues in 2007 dollars. . . . Worth noting are the new light-rail projects that have passed in what once appeared to be the most transit-averse states, such as those in the Mountain West, . . . including Arizona, Colorado, and Utah. In fact, the Denver region is building the largest light-rail system in the United States, while Salt Lake City is significantly expanding its transit and adding commuter-rail lines at the same time.[33]

Many of transit's success stories are occurring in the West: Voters in California, Hawaii, New Mexico, and Washington have recently approved big bumps upward in spending, usually by two-thirds margins. Small sales tax increases to support light-rail expansions were defeated in St. Louis and Kansas City.

Why is this so? Have preferences shifted more toward transit in western states than elsewhere? Is metropolitan governance stronger in western states because counties are larger and have more powers than do counties in the Northeast and Midwest? Less government fragmentation and more containment of metropolitan population within one state may contribute to organizational success in achieving public support, including means of financing transit from local, regional, and state funding sources.

Infrastructure investment, however, is only one need. There is a need to increase residential densities and create mixed use settings, with many activities near transit stations. While some jobs should be near transit stations, most workers will arrive via transit, having boarded at other stations. A majority of residences should be within walking, biking, or bus distances of shops, groceries, bakeries, restaurants, parks, schools, and places of worship. Those people will not have to drive for entire days. Diverse choices available nearby save time, increase options, add to feelings of influence and control, and reduce stress. They create eyes on the street for safe walking. They reduce driving, which produces 42,000 deaths and more than two million injuries each year.

Household spending on transportation averages 18 percent but varies by location. Outer suburban residents average

25 percent of household income for transportation, compared with only 9 percent for households in compact development settings.[34] Living amid sprawl raises transportation costs. The people most interested in compact settings are households with the youngest and oldest adults, including ones in which children no longer are living at home. One poll found that "77 percent of Americans born after 1981 want to live in an 'urban core.' . . . Another survey . . . found that 71 percent of [baby] boomers placed walking distance to transit at the top of their list of housing demands."[35] The numbers of baby boomers and elderly are growing fast, and both are likely to become stronger advocates for transit.

TRANSIT-ORIENTED DEVELOPMENT

Federal, state, and local transportation policies have not done enough to connect transportation and land use. Federal and state transit funds should be spent in areas where local governments collaborate in planning transit investments; organize to provide a dedicated source of funds for operations, in addition to fares; and adapt land use controls to encourage the location of lots of people near stations in suburbs as well as in cities.

A risk associated with required collaboration among local governments could be that suburbs' representatives will support highway spending that encourages more sprawl. With many central cities constituting small proportions of metropolitan populations, the possibility that MPOs will promote deconcentration is a significant danger. Collaboration is a means to an end. The goal should be more compact development, shorter routine trips, and more alternatives to driving alone. Collaboration itself is not the goal.

The Washington, D.C., and Atlanta areas implemented heavy-rail transit systems in the 1970s. Their experiences demonstrate the importance of local governments being committed to achieving higher residential densities and mixed use developments. Washington, D.C., and some suburban cities and counties planned for transit-oriented development, and use of transit rose to the second-highest level in the United States. Atlanta did little along these lines. Atlanta's transit use lagged, which may be one reason why Atlanta has the most declining suburbs in the country.

Within the Washington, D.C., metropolitan area, Alexandria, Arlington, and Montgomery counties emphasized transit-oriented development, and Fairfax and Prince George's Counties did not. Today, there is less density in Fairfax and Prince George's and more use of personal motor vehicles for routine daily activities, including commuting to work.[36] Alexandria, Arlington, and Montgomery have thrived.[37]

GLOBAL LOCALISM

Dealing with oil depletion and climate change in the United States requires decisions by individuals and households, governments at each level, private businesses, and nonprofit organizations. With decentralized private markets, countless producers of goods and services, and thousands of local governments, individuals' decisions will determine many outcomes, including influencing global business and national capacities.

From 1990 to 2009, many people changed direction when it came to where they wanted to live. In time, this could have major effects. Access and convenience became more important—they got more "votes." Large amounts of interior and exterior residential space got fewer "votes": sizes of new houses stabilized from 2005 through 2007.

The federal and state governments are not well positioned to determine acceptable or desirable patterns of development and redevelopment. They have little influence over development policies affecting houses, parcels, blocks, streets, neighborhoods, mixed use districts, downtowns, edge cities, and transit-oriented development. Citizens feel an intense need for a say in how their immediate surroundings are developed.

Ironically, local influence is an obstacle to achieving the goals that many people desire. Small units of local government and small districts within local governments for electing local council members and county board members seem best to many citizens, to help them control nearby development decisions. But these entities are much better suited to preventing more density in neighborhoods than to creating desirable places.

The ideal that people can and often should take 50 percent or more of their trips by means other than driving alone cannot be achieved unless citizens give up some influence on development near where they live. Even at small scale, therefore, governance adjustments are required to support, and to be supported by, decisions by individuals to alter their travel behavior, whether the motivation is self-interest (to reduce costs, improve health, and enhance quality of neighborhood life) or ethics (sharing the burden of saving the planet).

TYRANNY OF EASY DEVELOPMENT DECISIONS

Local governments must be leading partners in efforts to use transit to make better places and improve the quality of daily life.

While some constituents will see the logic of such an approach in relation to climate change, the tyranny of easy development decisions often will be an obstacle. One aspect of that tyranny is that neighbors often protest development, including transportation investments, near their residences. In the Atlanta area, some residents of northern suburbs opposed rail transit in the 1970s because they feared transit users were crime-prone and their neighborhoods would become less safe. In the suburbs of Richmond, Virginia, similar fears were expressed in the 1990s about bus service to suburban shopping centers. Bus riders were potential crime threats, some feared. Suburban elected officials in the Atlanta and Richmond areas paid attention to fearful people and did not make investments to benefit future rail transit and bus riders.

In the New Jersey suburbs of Philadelphia, violent crime fell from 2004 to 2007 in most towns after a light-rail line opened between Camden and Trenton. But fear of crime increases along a proposed light-rail line between Camden and Glassboro led one sheriff to seek a federal grant to cope with an anticipated increase in gang activity if the line was constructed.[38]

On the other hand, residents of Arlington, Virginia, participated in lengthy planning sessions from which plans emerged to transform the county with up to 10 transit-oriented development districts. These station areas evolved over a 30-year period into high-rise mixed use districts within approximately a quarter-mile of stations. They have continued to evolve according to generally agreed-upon plans. As fuel costs increase and examples of successful transit-oriented development become more familiar, more city and suburban areas will rally to the virtues of mixed use districts knitted together by transit.

Local elected officials will be more likely to try to overcome neighborhood opposition if they are encouraged by financial support from federal or state governments. With more than 100 governments per large metropolitan area and many more than that in many large metropolitan areas, the obstacles to metropolitan decision making are enormous. Local officials have difficulty justifying spending time on long-shot policies and projects when their in-baskets are full and staff support, especially in small suburbs, is scarce.

TRANSPORTATION PLANNING FOR RESULTS

Reducing nonrenewable energy consumption and greenhouse gas emissions depends on changes in the way people travel and changes in household locations, as well as moving jobs, shops, and homes closer to one another. Rail construction and express bus routes often require multilocal government collaborations that neither state nor local governments can mandate. More than 100 local governments per large metropolitan area mean that the time and effort for officials of any single government to launch a collaborative transportation and planning exercise is onerous. While local government cooperation in MPOs is required, reductions in energy consumption and greenhouse gas emissions are not.[39]

Federal transportation policy has been essentially without direction. It has mainly continued the highway construction emphasis embedded in the interstate highway program adopted by Congress in 1956. It is not linked tightly enough to today's new realities and what they imply by way of economic development: It is not aimed at enhancing seaport capacity to better compete with other nations in international trade. It is not aimed at reducing shipping costs by enhancing rail freight transportation. It is not aimed at reducing wasted time sitting at airports and traveling in cabs to and from airports instead of taking high-speed rail on business trips of 500 miles or less, as is the norm in Europe and Japan. It is not aimed at transit-oriented development to save time, reduce air pollution, limit sprawl, and enhance property values within metropolitan areas, where 80 percent of the population lives. And there is no national system for allocating funds among these goals, to the extent that such goals are embedded in priorities of any of the 50 states.

And it lacks an effective metropolitan focus. Although Congress has sought to give local officials more flexibility, metropolitan areas still had direct control over only 5.8 percent of federal highway spending from 1998 through 2002.[40] Consequently, federal transportation policy's main challenge is to create meaningful metropolitan goals and practices.

At metropolitan scale, the Brookings Institution's Blueprint for America has advocated two useful policies to support compact development and carbon emission reductions. The first policy is to stop favoring highways. Highways should be subject to multiple tests of potential effectiveness, just as transit is.[41] The second is what Brookings calls Sustainability Challenge Contracts. These contracts, it says,

> should be created to entice states and metropolitan areas to devise a broad vision for coping with congestion and greenhouse gas emissions across transportation, housing, land use, economic development and energy policies. . . . Partnerships of states, metropolitan areas, localities, and the private sector would apply for these competitive grants that would ideally encompass a range of solutions from all modes and would tie-in directly to an articulate set of national transportation outcomes. . . . Examples include household savings, accessibility/choices, climate goals, least cost infrastructure and others. . . . The federal government should fund most of the development of these plans (e.g. at an 80/20 split) in exchange for which official action should be taken by state legislatures and/or MPOs for official endorsement.[42]

Rather than basing transit funding decisions on "capital and operating costs divided by time saved," emphasis should be on stimulating "efficient high-density transit-oriented development. . . . [T]he federal government should remove the prohibition for dense concentrations of affordable units if they are within close proximity to transit stations . . . [which instead] should be encouraged."[43]

These two Brookings proposals point transportation policy in the correct direction and would unleash some creative local and metropolitan planning.

SUSTAINABLE REGION INCENTIVE PROGRAM

Additional steps to integrate planning, implementation, and evaluation also are needed but would face more obstacles in generating legislative support. A Sustainable Region Incentive Program (SRIP) should be designed to address limited metropolitan transportation and land development capabilities. An SRIP would be most effective with three components. The first component is some funding for planning. Planning should address transportation modes, paths, stations, land ownership, development management, residential density, and mixed use near stations. Planning should lead to project proposals and approvals by local governing bodies. These proposals and approvals should include management structures, reliable capital and operating finance, and land use controls that nurture adequate population density and mixed use development. These processes are complicated. Incentives to launch these processes will increase the number of metropolitan areas in which local governments are willing to collaborate on transportation and land use integration.

The second component is capital and operating funding. Some federal and state funding should be contingent on adequate local cost sharing of capital and operating expenses. Federal grants should require matching state as well as local funds. Most federal and state funds would be for multijurisdictional projects. The main reason for the SRIP process is coping with the complexity of multilocal government decision making. The SRIP should provide funding sufficient to generate serious multijurisdictional deliberations. Therefore, multilocal projects would be emphasized.

The third component of the SRIP, which supplements the Brookings recommendations, is rewards for results. Plans and projects are means to a goal. The goal is results. Therefore, results should be rewarded. Rewards can be transfer payments or priority funding for future projects. The federal government is the best source of reward funds because it is less constrained by unpredictable economic downturns than are states. States are required to have balanced budgets. State capital expenditures typically are reduced during recessions. The federal government usually operates with a deficit. The federal government can deliberately increase its deficit during recessions to increase consumer demand and employment. Consequently, the federal government can be a more reliable provider of rewards that will occur at least several years, or even a decade, after project investments have been completed.

Settling on appropriate result measures would be challenging. Result indicators could be straightforward, such as reaching a target number of public transit users. Result indicators also could be less direct, such as reducing the percentage of commuters who drive alone to work. Another could be reducing greenhouse gas emissions from transportation. Reducing vehicle miles traveled per person is the means to these results. Acquiring relevant data is a major research task. It will require federal or state funding.

These result indicators do not flow only from implementation of the project, such as creation or expansion of a heavy rail, light rail, or streetcar system or an express bus system. They are influenced by the pattern of land development and redevelopment, population density, job locations, and activities available close to peoples' homes. Therefore, rewards for results can motivate changes in development planning, zoning, guidance for developers, individuals' travel behavior, and residential location decisions.

ACCOUNTING FOR BEHAVIOR, SCALE, AND INCENTIVES

People choose to use transit, to bicycle, to walk, or to drive alone. People who have always driven alone for errands and entertainment can decide walking is a form of entertainment as well as exercise. In 2001, about one trip in four was one mile or less. Yet only about one in five of these short trips was made on foot. A program called Healthy People 2010 aims to increase this to one in four trips of one mile or less.[44] Consequently, education and persuasion can be aspects of reaching SRIP goals. If SRIP goals can be reached through more behavior change and private land use development relative to public infrastructure investments, rewards would be warranted.

A multijurisdictional SRIP strategy may not be required. But federal and state project funds should be available to encourage capital expenditures, for example, for streetcar lines contained within a single jurisdiction, streets that access well-located brownfield sites, and pedestrian settings that attract high-density residences.

Projects intended to increase walking and transit use have not always qualified for state or federal transportation funds. Take for instance a road project in Charlottesville, Virginia. The extension of Water Street, on the south side of downtown, through a mostly abandoned railroad yard to a perpendicular street east of downtown has helped increase downtown population density, promote mixed use development, and clean up a polluted site. It added three significant employers of hundreds of office and research workers in the railyard, two four-story residential condominiums, and proposals for 500 condominiums and attached single-unit residences east of downtown, plus an additional extension of Water Street to be built by a developer. All of these jobs and residences were amenable to walking and transit. But the Virginia Department of Transportation contributed zero dollars because the project did not qualify as a primary arterial or secondary collector. From the perspective of global warming and nonrenewable resource depletion, it was by far the most useful project in 40 years of transportation expenditures in the Charlottesville area. State and federal transportation priorities need to change to deal with 21st-century issues.

Federal transportation programs include perverse incentives. States qualify for more federal funds, for example, if their vehicle miles increase.[45] Incentives should be the opposite, as they were in the Senate version of the federal transportation bill of 1991. The Senate would have reduced a state's allocation if vehicle miles per person increased 10 percent or more. Withheld funds would have been set aside to reward states in which travel went down by 10 percent or more.[46]

The Clean Air Act Amendments of 1990 include potential transportation funding penalties for metropolitan areas exceeding pollutant emission standards. If plans fail to demonstrate how the pollutant levels will be reduced, federal transportation funds can be withheld. Although 63 metropolitan areas had lapses in meeting pollution standards related to vehicle emissions by 2004, no state had lost federal transportation funds.[47] Poor performance should lead to lower priority for federal transportation funds, especially for highways. Performance achievements should be rewarded from a separate funding source, such as an SRIP fund, especially for transit.

ENERGY USE IN BUILDINGS

While transportation and land use require large-scale action, energy use and CO_2 emissions from buildings can be managed one building at a time. Transportation accounted for 28 percent of energy use in the United States in 2007. Buildings accounted for 39 percent—21 percent in residences and 18 percent in commercial buildings.[48]

Arguing for a large renovation and energy-conservation component of the 2009 federal Economic Stimulus Package, Edward Mazria and Kristina Kershner said that the private building sector constitutes 93 percent of U.S. buildings, making it more important than public infrastructure to economic recovery.[49] They advocated mortgage interest writedowns to as low as 2.5 percent in exchange for energy-reduction specifications 75 percent more stringent than standard building-code requirements. By using the mortgage interest-rate carrot, individual property owners could be motivated to renovate in energy-efficient ways, reviving the economy and reducing energy use. Federal government action would not need to be integrated with either state or local government actions to achieve results.

This example embodies the strength and weakness of building-focused policies. They can be stimulated by action by any level of government. Federal government policies can be effective nationwide. Federally chartered agencies like Fannie Mae, Freddie Mac, and the Federal Housing Administration are experienced in administering mortgage transactions one owner and one building at a time.

Reducing energy use in buildings depends upon owners who are sufficiently motivated to invest in reducing energy. Even at low interest rates, remodeling to reduce monthly costs by using less energy has uncertain prospects. Renovations encounter problems. Walls, windows, floors, roofs, and doors must be tightened. Many owners will be skeptical about the likelihood of success. Being skeptical, renovating with current income rather than borrowed money—insulating walls and replacing leaky windows one side of house at a time—will seem wiser financially. But such a process will yield modest rewards in reduced energy costs until every wall and window segment has been upgraded. Competing uses for the same dollars may have more support in the household. For these reasons, energy-focused renovations will lag behind national needs.

Weatherization grant programs, therefore, will attract more participants. Weatherization programs usually are aimed at low- and moderate-income home owners who cannot afford to borrow for energy upgrades at market rates. They cost more in federal dollars per renovation than giving tax credits to home owners who borrow or use current income. Who qualifies to participate is an issue. To limit costs, weatherization programs typically are combined with affordable housing goals. By reducing energy use, housing becomes more affordable in any price range. For most local governments, distributing weather-ization benefits to a limited number of home owners in certain income categories stretches their financial capacity without clear rationale for distinguishing between potential beneficiaries. Fairness as well as cost is an issue. And, as with house-holds, local governments face many competing worthwhile uses for scarce funds. Other funding priorities will limit local government weatherization investments.

ENERGY SAVINGS IN NEW BUILDINGS

Energy use and greenhouse gas emission reductions are easier to achieve in new buildings than by renovating existing buildings or by integrating transportation and land development. Rather than involving reductions in auto-dependent lifestyles, a building focus involves changes in construction that can be executed within the same building envelopes and same locations to which consumers have grown accustomed. They may include some increases in construction costs for equipment (solar panels, point-of-use hot water, double- and triple-pane windows, more effective insulation, Styrofoam steel construction). They do not threaten the American way of life as do changes in transportation and land use.

Energy-efficient new building construction has major energy-saving potential. Arthur Nelson has estimated that "over half of development on the ground in 2025 will not have existed in 2000."[50] Looking farther ahead to 2037, when the U.S. population may reach 400 million, Nelson and Robert Lang estimated that 70 million new housing units will have been built: 40 million for the additional 100 million people and 30 million replacements for demolished housing units.[51] That suggests huge potential for reducing energy use and greenhouse gas emissions per unit. But it also indicates the potential increase in energy and emissions if the nation doesn't aggressively pursue green methods.

States can require certain construction products and practices through building and housing codes. Local governments can be partners through inspections that review construction for compliance and zoning ordinances that affect solar orientation and shade. But local governments strapped for funds have little reason to emphasize inspections and may worry that zoning requirements will impede development. State aid targeted for inspections, state technical assistance for local regulations, and state rewards for achieving energy and greenhouse gas reductions from buildings could increase local government collaboration. Focus on residential and commercial buildings would be a relatively simple collaborative task, because state agencies can assign tasks to individual local governments rather than be dependent on multilocal government collaboration to achieve transportation and land use goals.

States can authorize powers for local governments to apply to green building. In Maryland, for example, Montgomery County, adjacent to Washington, D.C., announced its intention to become the nation's first local government to require that new single-family residences meet the federal Environmental Protection Agency's Energy Star efficiency standards. Estimated cost increases of $2,000 to $20,000 per residence, depending on size, would achieve energy savings of 15 to 30 percent. Developers and builders can be fined for failure to comply.[52]

Unless states make sure there are uniform energy requirements, local governments such as Montgomery County, confident of their ability to attract new home buyers, or local governments wishing to prevent construction of new residences are most likely to act separately from their peers. Most local governments will lack sufficient incentives to impose such requirements. State mandates for uniformity are better.

Stronger metropolitan governance can help, because it reduces local competition for property tax base. If property tax competition was reduced, local—or metropolitan—regulation of building characteristics reducing nonrenewable energy use can be enhanced.

Ultimately, building code requirements and energy prices will drive use of energy in buildings. Code requirements will determine energy use of most new buildings. Motivated buyers and builders sometimes will exceed code requirements. Prices will play a role in new buildings, because energy-conscious new construction is easier and more cost effective than energy-motivated renovations.

Prices, mainly, will drive energy-motivated renovations. Because renovations are expensive and outcomes are more difficult to predict than with new construction, high prices for energy will motivate more renovation. Low-cost loan programs and tax deductions or tax credits for major investments like solar heating will be useful supplements to effects of high prices. With each of these types of programs, federal and state governments will have major roles. Local governments will be minor players. The absence of effective metropolitan governments can be overcome, because the main decision makers are households and the facilities are individual buildings.

CONCLUSION

The sprawl, energy, transportation, and climate connection runs through people—you and me. We decide what to do. Reducing energy use through transportation can be promoted by public transit investments and with local plans for compact development. Those plans are more likely to be made, and transit investments are more likely, if we ask for them—and if we vote for them with our feet and with our checkbooks. Such decisions have been occurring more often. The next step is for people who have been choosing convenient places to live, and those who so aspire, to speak politically.

NOTES

1. U.S. Energy Information Administration (EIA), *Annual Energy Review, Energy Consumption by Sector, Selected Years, 1949–2006* (Washington, D.C.: U.S. Department of Energy, 2008), 38.
2. Pew Center on Global Climate Change, "GHG Emissions by Sector" (2008), Diagram 4B; available at www.pewclimate.org/global-warming-basics/facts_and_figures.
3. In 2005, the figure was 30.5 percent. U.S. EIA, *Annual Energy Review*, 145. Some petroleum is used in industrial products, such as plastics, and in products for agriculture like fertilizer.
4. From 3,419 thousand barrels per day in 1970 to 6,909 in 1980, 8,018 in 1990, 11,459 in 2000, and 13,714 in 2005, an increase of 10,395 thousand barrels per day.
5. From 14,697 thousand barrels per day in 1970 to 17,056 in 1980, 16,988 in 1990, 19,701 in 2000, and 20,802 in 2005. U.S. EIA, *Annual Energy Review*, 125.
6. From 9,637 thousand barrels per day in 1970 to 5,178 in 2005. Ibid.
7. U.S. Bureau of Transportation Statistics (BTS), *National Transportation Statistics* (Washington, D.C.: U.S. Department of Transportation [DOT], 2008), Tables 4-9, 4-12.

8. Bill Marsh, "Burning through Oil or Conserving It," *New York Times*, April 20, 2008, Week in Review section.
9. U.S. BTS, *Freight in America* (Washington, D.C.: U.S. DOT, 2006).
10. European Environment Agency, "Climate for a Transport Change," EEA Report No. 1/2008, 2008, 52; U.S. BTS, *National Transportation Statistics*, Table 4-A.
11. Metropolitan Policy Program, *A Bridge to Somewhere: Rethinking American Transportation for the 21st Century* (Washington, D.C.: Brookings Institution, 2008), 62.
12. Reid Ewing, Keith Bartholomew, Steve Winkelman, Jerry Walters, and Don Chen, *Growing Cooler: The Evidence on Urban Development and Climate Change* (Washington, D.C.: Urban Land Institute, 2008), 113.
13. Center for Urban Transportation Research, "Public Transit in America: Results from the 2001 National Household Travel Survey" (Tampa, Fla.: National Center for Transit Research, University of South Florida, 2005).
14. Person trips averaged four per day in 2001. Sandra A. Ham, Caroline A. Macera, and Corine Lindley, "Trends in Walking for Transportation in the United States, 1995 and 2001" (2005), *Preventing Chronic Disease* 2, 4; available at www.cdc.gov/pcd/issues/2005/oct/04_0138.htm. Average household size was 2.6 persons in 2000.
15. U.S. Bureau of Census, "American Community Survey 2005" (and 2006), American Factfinder Data Profiles, 2007, Economic Data. Commuting accounts for about 20 percent of all trips per household. Trip mode data are not available in the census for other trips.
16. U.S. Bureau of Census, "Census of Population and Housing 2000" (and 1990), American Factfinder, 2008, Detailed Tables, Means of Transportation to Work.
17. Ewing et al., *Growing Cooler*, 68.
18. Vaclav Smil, "Driving and Fuel Consumption," 2008; available at http://home.cc.umanitoba.ca/~vsmil/graphics/energy/fueldistance.htm.
19. European Environment Agency, "Climate for a Transport Change," 8.
20. Transportation Information Sources, *TDM Encyclopedia* (2007), Table 1; available at www.vtpi.org/tdm/tdm80.htm.
21. Timothy Beatley, *Green Urbanism: Learning from European Cities* (Washington, D.C.: Island Press, 2000).

22. U.S. Bureau of Labor Statistics, *Consumer Price Index Components* (Washington, D.C.: U.S. Department of Labor, 2008).
23. Eurostat, "Household Budget Survey in 2005 in EU27" (2008); available at http://ec.europa.eu/eurostat.
24. Peter Newman and Jeffrey Kenworthy, *Sustainability and Cities* (Washington, D.C.: Island Press, 1999).
25. Wendell Cox, "Debunking Friday the 13th: 13 Myths of Urban Sprawl" (Heartland Institute, 2003); available at www.heartland .org.
26. Metropolitan population densities decreased from an average of 50 persons per hectare in 1995 to 47 in 2001. This density decline was matched by a decline in the share of trips by transit, walking, and cycling from 50.0 to 47.5 percent. In the United States, 13.1 percent of commuter trips in 2000 were by transit, walking, and cycling (including the 3.3 percent who worked at home), down from 13.4 percent in 1990 (including 3.0 percent who worked at home).
27. Marilyn A. Brown, Frank Southworth, and Andrea Sarzynski, *Shrinking the Carbon Footprint of Metropolitan America* (Washington, D.C.: Brookings Institution Metropolitan Policy Program, 2008).
28. Metropolitan Policy Program, *Bridge to Somewhere*, 8
29. U.S. BTS, *National Transportation Statistics*, Table 4-A.
30. Edward Beimborn and Robert Puentes, "Highways and Transit: Leveling the Playing Field in Federal Transportation Policy," in *Taking the High Road: A Metropolitan Agenda for Transportation Reform*, ed. Bruce Katz and Robert Puentes (Washington, D.C.: Brookings Institution, 2005), 269. Of transit expenditures in 2001, 21 percent were from federal revenues, with 79 percent from state and local government revenues. The federal share of capital investments in transit (39 percent) has nearly doubled the federal share of all transit expenditures, including operating expenditures. States (13 percent), local governments (22 percent), and transit agencies (27 percent) provided the remaining 61 percent of transit capital expenditures. See Cambridge Systematics, *State and National Transit Investment Analysis* (Washington, D.C.: American Association of State Highway and Transportation Officials, 2007), Table 40.
31. Cambridge Systematics, *State and National Transit Investment Analysis*.
32. Associated Press, "$50 Billion Needed to Fix Rail Transit, Study Says," www.msnbc.com, April 30, 2009.

33. Arthur C. Nelson and Robert E. Lang, *The New Politics of Planning* (Washington, D.C.: Urban Land Institute, 2009), 18. Referenda on authorizations of, or sales taxes for, regional, county, and city transit expansion proposals mainly were successful in November 2008. Voters in 16 states approved 23 of 32 (72 percent) state and local public transit-related referenda. See National Association of Railroad Passengers, "Hotline #578," November 7, 2008.

34. Shelley Poticha, "Reconnecting America with Transit," presentation at the Congress of the New Urbanism seminar, Dallas, March 31, 2009.

35. Alan Ehrenhalt, "Putting the Urban in Suburban," *Governing*, March 9–10, 2009, 9.

36. Robert Cervero, *The Transit Metropolis* (Washington, D.C.: Island Press, 1998).

37. William H. Lucy and David L. Phillips, *Confronting Suburban Decline* (Washington, D.C.: Island Press, 2000).

38. Paul Nussbaum, "Not All Are Aboard in Glouco: Will Light Rail Bring Crime?" *Philadelphia Inquirer*, May 25, 2009.

39. Katz and Puentes, *Taking the High Road*.

40. Robert Puentes and Linda Bailey, "Increasing Funding and Accountability for Metropolitan Transportation Decisions," in Katz and Puentes, *Taking the High Road*, 144.

41. Metropolitan Policy Program, *Bridge to Somewhere*, 8.

42. Ibid., 66.

43. Ibid., 68.

44. Ham et al., "Trends in Walking."

45. Ewing et al., *Growing Cooler*, 129.

46. Ibid., 132.

47. Ibid., 136.

48. U.S. EIA, *Annual Energy Review, Energy Consumption by Sector, Selected Years, 1949–2007* (Washington, D.C.: U.S. Department of Energy, 2009), 38.

49. Edward Mazria and Kristina Kershner, "Architecture 2030: The Two-Year, Nine-Million-Jobs Investment" (January 2009); available at www.architecture2030.org.

50. Arthur C. Nelson, "Leadership in a New Era," *Journal of the American Planning Association* 72, no. 4 (2006): 393–407.

51. Arthur C. Nelson and Robert E. Lang, "The Next 100 Million," *Planning*, January 2007, 4.

52. Ann E. Marimow, "Montgomery Aims to Make Green Homes Mandatory," *Washington Post*, April 23, 2008.

5

The Outmoded Metropolis

One of the virtues of learning a foreign language is that it makes us conscious of the *connotations* of words, as well as their meanings. The English word "suburb," for instance, translates into French as *"banlieue,"* or outskirts. But the connotations of the two words are precisely the opposite.

> While some wealthy cities and desirable neighborhoods do exist in the outskirt of Paris and other big cities, in French *"banlieue"* automatically evokes the image of housing projects, with young people hanging around wearing baseball caps and sweatsuits, smoking joints, perhaps standing beside a burning car. *"Banlieues"* have become the symbol of a bleak urban environment, deviant youth and segregated minorities, whereas "suburb" in the United States designates quiet, wealthy areas, with nice, large houses and white middle- or upper-class families.[1]

Quite so. And the danger Americans face today is of these two words, suburb and *banlieue*, ceasing to be the opposite and beginning to become the same. Much as the left in particular, together with downtown business interests, has yearned for a revival at the center, it is not going to be a good thing for this country to start heading toward a Frenchified world of culturally rich and aesthetically pleasing central business districts coupled with decaying, crime-ridden suburbs. And so the thing to consider is what is to be done to keep vulnerable suburbs healthy.

One major problem American suburbs face is their fragmentation: their itsy-bitsy size. A city of, say, 10 square miles made a lot more sense back when we walked or rode horseback, and we didn't routinely travel long distances. But streetcars, buses, and cars rendered many boundaries obsolete. True, some cities grew by annexing surrounding areas or merging with other entities. But in many other cases we are stuck with boundaries dating from a previous age.

After World War II, the dominance of automobiles, population growth, new and wider highways, and rising affluence sped suburbanization in pursuit of an American dream of owning a home with an ample yard. Neither annexation nor consolidation kept up with the speed and scope of suburban expansion.

Government officials adapted mainly by creating "special districts," which allowed jurisdictions to band together to do some things that would have been insane to undertake on their own. Constructing airports and landfills were particularly obvious cases, but water, sewers, transit, and other sectors were involved. Between 1952 and 2002, the number of special districts shot from 12,340 to 35,052.[2]

These districts, operating alongside the traditional cities, counties, towns, townships, and villages, meant a bewildering array of bodies—too many for the average person to even be aware of, much less evaluate as wise or unwise. Where was one to go to ask about a stop sign? A broken water main? Broken swings at playgrounds? More computers at libraries? Property assessments or taxes?

Libertyville, Illinois, with population of about 20,000, is a particularly stark example. It has 13 government entities to which local taxes are paid. Officials solved the billing problem by consolidating all the taxes owed into a single bill. But that did not answer the question about where to direct complaints and requests for services. As to whether services were efficient, effective, or equitable—who knew? And who knew whom to blame if they were not?

And on a much larger scale, what about decisions as to how an entire metropolitan area was to grow? Whoever consciously decided that sprawl was the way to go? Any attempt within a city to create a multistory building on a bus line met with scathing public reactions: as a left-wing state legislator in Minneapolis once put it, in a conversation with a reporter, "Just try to put an apartment building at 54th and Lyndale [enlightened, Green Party, scooter-riding territory] and you'd think you were in Maple Grove [a suburb renowned for its opposition to affordable housing]!"

Development opportunities were more prevalent on the fringe of metropolitan areas. There, public officials, tending to associate growth with prosperity, many of them bankers or real estate agents themselves, supported growth. Suburban and exurban sprawl ensued.

Few citizens were willing to, or showed interest in, limiting or guiding land development patterns. Fragmentation frustrated efforts to generate metropolitan visions of a desirable future. Cities competed for tax base.

But metropolitan areas were not organized to provide effective services for many citizens. Richer places had fewer needs; poorer places had greater needs. There was often a surprising amount of deterioration in a new suburb just two or three decades after it was built out.

That is where metropolitan areas are today. They can't create or renew basic services and facilities where they are most needed. They don't work together enough. They have antiquated local tax structures. In baseball terms, they are playing "small ball"—bunting, stealing a base here and there—instead of hitting home runs. When you are way behind, when it comes to coping with climate change and oil depletion, home runs are necessary.

Perhaps the greatest hope for change in this sprawl pattern stems from the combined impact of these two looming disasters: climate change, which means we must limit CO_2 emissions, and the prospect of an end to cheap oil. Together these threats mean we must change the way we get around and the way we distribute homes and offices and stores across the landscape. Metropolitan areas have an indispensable role in making these changes. But their governance structure, powers, and traditions are inadequate for the task.

This chapter suggests means of coping with these limitations. Although more metropolitan governance capacity would be extremely helpful, fortunately some useful actions pertinent to climate change and oil depletion do not require creating new metropolitan governments.

REGIONAL METROPOLITANISM

Some national climate change and oil depletion policies can be brought about without parallel actions by state and local governments. An assertive national agenda can be made real through subsidies for technological innovations (biomass energy sources and more effective electricity transmission), producer mandates (gas-mileage targets for motor-vehicle fleets and renewable electric power sources), and producer incentives (cap-and-trade systems to limit carbon-dioxide emissions). Some parts of an aggressive agenda can be addressed through incentives for households (tax credits for solar panel installations) and raising taxes on those with high incomes. Some parts can be carried out interactively: incentives for solar panels on homes, even as electric power companies are made to accept that electricity into their distribution systems.

Local governments dominate land use, but federal regulation of water and air influence land use in many locations. States act at times as federal government partners and delegate land use powers to local governments whose territories may be as small as a few square miles in some states (suburbs of Philadelphia and Pittsburgh are cases in point) or thousands of square miles in others (Riverside and San Bernardino counties, outside Los Angeles). Federal and state policies have helped clean up polluted water and prevent damage to wildlife. Additional federal policies will be needed to prevent egregious damage to the planet's atmosphere from CO_2 and other emissions. States can act directly to reduce nonrenewable energy use through policies similar to federal policies and by investing, planning, and building roads, transit, and energy-efficient buildings.

Many reductions in nonrenewable energy use in transportation and buildings, however, take effort by local governments, households, builders, and developers.

Metropolitan governance is a weak link in this network of collaborations. There are no directly elected general-purpose metropolitan governments in the United States. Portland, Oregon, comes closest: Metro Portland influences planning, land use, development, transportation, parks, and recycling. Metropolitan Minneapolis–St. Paul shares 40 percent of industrial and commercial revenues added after 1974 to the property tax base, but its Metropolitan Council, appointed by the governor and tasked with overseeing regional development, is not taken seriously as a force limiting sprawl.

Metropolitan areas contained within one or two counties, such as San Diego, Las Vegas, Phoenix, and Buffalo, can become effective at "metropolitan" government through county mechanisms. In metropolitan areas in states where annexation by central cities is common, primarily North Carolina, the central city can take charge of large portions of the metropolitan area, as Charlotte did.

More typical, though, is fragmentation. Large metropolitan areas average well over 100 local governments.[3] Collaboration becomes exceedingly difficult. Moreover, central cities rarely constitute more than 30 percent of population in large metropolitan areas. Many are smaller: 10 and 20 percent in Atlanta, Pittsburgh, San Francisco, St. Louis, and Washington, D.C.

Metropolitan areas are not well organized for two essential tasks.

First, they are organized so that they make worse rather than better the mismatch of needs and resources. Already in 2000 there were 155 suburbs where incomes of residents relative to mean and median metropolitan incomes were lower than incomes in the poorest central city, Detroit, relative to its metropolitan incomes.[4] This mismatch will shift as more central cities revive, becoming richer. Disparities among suburbs will increase: some will continue to thrive while many others decline, sometimes precipitously.

Second, most metropolitan areas lack organizations with sufficient authority to plan, finance, develop, and expand public transportation. And they lack authority to integrate transportation, land use, and land development. The federal government insists that metros coordinate their transportation planning through so-called metropolitan planning organizations (MPOs). But these are often organizations of elected officials representing local governments. They lack operating responsibilities. They plan transportation, but they can't plan land use or impose taxes. Robert Puentes and Linda Bailey have observed:

> Within many regions, local governments continue to compete with one another for their share of the metropolitan pie. In still other metropolitan areas, center cities, older suburbs, and minorities are underrepresented on MPO boards.[5]

In the past these deficiencies of metropolitan governance have been noted, lamented, and accepted. But in an era of climate change and an end to cheap oil, metropolitan disorganization becomes more dangerous: it frustrates effective responses.

Local governments don't want to give up power. Voters also have been reluctant to diminish their own influence, which is magnified when they have small units of local government. In the future, however, deficiencies stemming from small size may threaten the economic, political, and environmental viability of some metropolitan areas and collectively damage states and the nation.

SMART GROWTH AND STATES

States are the best metropolitan governments available, but they are not very good. Smart growth and growth management have been state efforts to limit sprawl. With sprawl culture dominant, although challenged, state efforts have been half-hearted and compromised.

Smart growth usually refers to efforts to reduce sprawl patterns, increase compact development, and increase use of alternatives to driving alone. There's evidence of an uptick in the number of elected state officials favoring smart growth. In Virginia, for example, Tim Kaine campaigned for governor in 2005 in favor of more integration of transportation and land use planning. In 2007, at Governor Kaine's behest, the General Assembly unanimously approved modifying state road-maintenance agreements to require more connectivity within subdivisions and between two or more subdivisions before the Department of Transportation would agree to maintain the subdivisions' streets. In March 2009, the department issued regulations requiring subdivisions to have two or more entrances and exits, permitting interior streets to be 24 to 29 feet wide instead of 36 to 40 feet, penalizing cul-de-sacs in a formula requiring more internal connectivity, internal sidewalks, and bicycle and pedestrian path connections to areas outside subdivisions.[6]

But the track record of states when it comes to smart growth goals has been mixed. In some respects, fragmentation of local governance related to growth management has been increasing. Arthur Nelson and Robert Lang have documented several instances before and since 2000.[7] The number of single-purpose special districts providing sewer, water, and solid waste services, airports, highways, or parks increased 10 percent from 1992 to 2002. The number of special districts for water and sewerage increased by 5 percent. States relied more on home owners' associations to provide services, including street, water, and sewer infrastructure, especially in high-growth states such as Arizona and Florida. State constitutional amendments and propositions limiting local governments' eminent-domain rights to acquire property for economic development were adopted in 10 states after the *Kelo* decision of the U.S. Supreme Court in 2005. On the other hand, between 1994 and 2006, 77 percent of smart growth–related referenda for acquiring parkland and financing public transit passed. More states also required state review of local plans and authorized more local plan elements. And the number of acres of land protected from development, mainly through conservation easements, nearly doubled from 2000 to 2005.

Maryland's Smart Growth program, promoted by Governor Parris Glendening in 1997, was one of the most ambitious efforts to integrate state and local planning. It featured local governments designating growth areas and the state targeting capital investments for schools, roads, water, and sewer into growth areas. The problem with this approach was that local governments created very large growth areas.[8] Reductions in vehicle miles and greenhouse gas emissions were not likely to result. After Glendening's two terms, his successor deemphasized some of these smart growth policies, due in part to a lack of funds.[9] Scholars at the National Center for Smart Growth Research and Education concluded: "There is no evidence after 10 years that [smart growth laws] have had any effect on development patterns." Three-fourths of single-unit houses were built outside locally designated smart-growth areas, which was the same percentage as before smart-growth laws were passed in 1997.[10]

California led other states in linking transportation, land use, and global warming by adopting the Global Warming Solutions Act of 2006. The legislation proposed smart growth goals, supported by $40 billion in infrastructure bonds to encourage compact development patterns. Voluntary regional targets, including limits on vehicle mile growth, were anticipated. California has a history of supporting transit. Since 1998, California alone among the 50 states has directed federal air-quality-improvement funds to MPOs, which then allocated 21 percent of these discretionary funds to transit from 1998 through 2002.[11]

California does not have metropolitan governments, which complicates the setting of regional targets called for in its Global Warming Solutions Act. California has two other major metropolitan governance problems. In passing Proposition 13 in 1978, voters stripped local governments of many of the property taxes they would otherwise have received by limiting assessment increases to 2 percent per year. Cutbacks in local services ensued. Service deficiencies have been a norm since 1978 in many jurisdictions.[12] Inadequate local revenues led to heavy reliance on home owners associations to provide infrastructure, including streets, in new subdivisions. Most new housing in California has been of that type.[13] New associations were particularly hard hit by the foreclosure crisis of 2008 and 2009. The associations add another layer of regional fragmentation and, when underfunded, can be another obstacle to regional collaboration.

California's policies to reduce CO_2 emissions must cope with a local government structure that is not able to perform routine governance functions effectively. California's Global Warming Solutions Act attempts to deal with an emergent problem that was not envisioned when Proposition 13 was approved. Global warming was not a perceived problem when California began relying on home owners associations to compensate for atrophied local governments. California's demands on local governments from global warming concerns are somewhat analogous to cutting off someone's feet and hands and then offering to train them to run a four-minute mile and become a concert pianist. Worse still, the state legislature was unable to agree for months on a state budget in 2009, because of a requirement that tax-increase bills achieve a two-thirds majority.[14]

Overall, state growth management has not noticeably increased compact development or reduced sprawl. A recent summary of state and local growth management did not cite evidence that these policies had overcome sprawl trends.[15]

COPING WITH MISMATCH OF NEEDS AND RESOURCES

Low- and moderate-resource local governments lack financial and staff capability to participate effectively in transit transformation. This is another reason why state governments should address the problem of the mismatch itself. Means of addressing this can be direct and indirect. State aid formulas, especially for public education, often are need-based in part. Aid formulas often include more state aid for local school districts with low revenue capacity and perhaps for students from low-income households. State aid formulas for specific functions—such as local jails, courts, public hospitals, and homeless shelters—may reward shared facilities between local governments. Rewards for sharing facilities can increase incentives for fiscally strong local governments to collaborate with fiscally weaker local governments.

State governments can influence local revenue sharing. States can mandate it. In Minnesota, the state legislature established a program of sharing with the seven major metropolitan counties around Minneapolis and St. Paul involving 40 percent of property-tax revenues from new industrial and commercial development. The formula has tended to assist low- and moderate-income suburbs rather than helping the central cities.[16] The Twin Cities was the only U.S. metro area in which the income range between the richest and poorest suburbs stayed the same rather than widening from 1960 to 1990.[17]

States also can determine the redistribution formulas for sales taxes collected by counties and distributed to cities, towns, villages, boroughs, and school districts. Sales taxes can be distributed to the local jurisdiction of origin, which tends to benefit central cities with successful downtowns and suburbs containing major edge cities. On the other hand, sales taxes can be distributed based partially on population or property tax base, with higher population and lower tax-base jurisdictions receiving more.

States establish procedures for incorporation and consolidation. Incorporation can be easy, ending up with numerous small jurisdictions. Consolidation can be rewarded with more state aid, which will encourage small jurisdictions to join together. Sometimes anomalies occur, such as on Long Island, in New York, where it seems state laws promoted two opposite local-government-incorporation outcomes. Long Island has two counties, Nassau and Suffolk, and Nassau is divided into only three towns. But Long Island also has 124 school districts with 659 schools, about five schools per district.

Why so many school districts? One can hypothesize that small school districts were inducements to development, creating opportunities for new home buyers to control school districts they shared with similarly situated households. Some school districts became dominated by low-income and minority households. The usual consequence of mismatch of needs and resources occurred. Low student performance has been concentrated in the

Long Island school districts with large percentages of low-income households with children eligible for free lunches.[18]

Once local governments are established, some local constituencies become committed to their preservation and to their own role in local affairs. Wealthy jurisdictions typically resist collaborating with poor jurisdictions. Even low-income jurisdictions resist losing powers, often based on an argument that their constituents' needs may be ignored in a larger jurisdiction. Thus, poor jurisdictions often resist consolidations also. Future residents do not speak up for the virtues of developments that have not yet occurred. Since consolidation has not occurred, any comparison of pre- and postconsolidation conditions is speculative rather than empirical or historical. Supporters of the status quo find persuasion easier, even if the status quo itself causes a lot of problems.

ENHANCING GOVERNANCE CAPABILITIES WITH TRANSIT AND REVENUE SHARING

The most direct path to reducing nonrenewable-energy consumption and greenhouse gas emissions in buildings and transportation is to reduce residential operating costs and improve places where residents want to walk and can use public transit. If local governments are well positioned within current residential location trends, they will be more able to pursue those goals effectively in the future.

But many local governments are deficient in the basic capabilities of governance. Their capacity to pursue their self-interest, and their constituents' self-interest, effectively is limited and often declining. Small, declining suburbs will have an especially difficult time. Lacking resources and being out of view and concern of major local government and economic decision makers, small low- and moderate-income middle-aged suburbs will continue to decline in their capabilities.

Some low-income cities and inner suburbs will begin to make comebacks if they have rail transit systems that can be revived through reinvestment. Their state governments may step in to support them, although having only 13 percent of transit capital costs coming from states in recent years is not an auspicious start. The federal government eventually will increase capital contributions to local and metropolitan transit systems. The federal government can increase capital investment in transit without confronting auto overdependence directly. Supporting existing transit systems is simple compared with the obstacles to creating new rail transit.

TWO OPTIONS FOR DECLINING SUBURBS

Unless a suburb's location is exceptional, the regional market is strong, and sprawl continues at a rapid pace, obstacles to reinvestment in small middle-aged houses will be daunting. But any local government, or a coalition of local governments, can assist with reinvestment challenges. Local government coalitions in Cuyahoga County surrounding Cleveland and in several counties surrounding Kansas City, Missouri, have begun this effort. Cuyahoga County has emphasized low-cost loans for expansions. Kansas City's suburbs have emphasized design manuals explaining realistic options for expanding the four main post–World War II house types. Suburban sprawl development has been driven by desires for four-bedroom houses. Some expansions of 1,100-square-foot average 1950 houses will reduce sprawl tendencies and enhance the property-tax assessments of declining suburbs.

The most likely local policy to aid in this effort, however, is the one that is easiest administratively but is least effective. That easy-to-implement policy is tax abatements for expansions that add more than a specified value to the property. This policy has two problems. One problem is that it does not add to the property-tax base for a number of years—and enhanced property-tax value is one motivation for the policy. The second problem is that it may not add to the number of house expansions that would have occurred without the tax abatement. Potential house expanders need assistance with front-end decisions, with construction implementation, and with up-front financing. Avoiding higher property taxes, after solving these problems, is desirable for home owners, but it does not directly address the more difficult decisions that precede construction. The strength of the Cuyahoga County and Kansas

City suburbs' efforts is that they are aimed at increasing loans for house expansions and providing design guidance to ease entry to the stressful remodeling effort.

SUBURBAN DOWNTOWNS, SHOPPING CENTERS, AND HOUSING

Focusing economic development effort on downtowns and bypassed shopping centers probably is the most typical suburban policy. These efforts are most likely to achieve political support. Success, if it can be achieved, will lead to the largest increase in property-tax revenues.[19] But success usually will be elusive. And success in these traditional economic development efforts will not be sufficient.

Residential rehabilitation and expansion are essential because residences comprise large proportions of suburban property-tax capacity. Consequently, suburbs that are out of what Christopher Leinberger calls "the favored quarter" where most owners of major businesses live—which tend to lack major conveniences like heavy rail and light-rail stations and which lack major assets like colleges and universities—will have great difficulty in attracting sufficient housing reinvestment.[20] Public policy inventions and interventions are needed, such as those attempted in Cuyahoga County and in suburbs near Kansas City, where 130 loans were made in the first two years of a low-cost loan program in inner suburbs.[21]

REBUILDING ACCESSIBILITY AND NATURE

As residents sort themselves increasingly by the attraction of convenience, accessible mixed use districts will induce more affluent residents to choose residences in central cities and some suburbs, especially suburbs with frequent transit connections to employment and entertainment.[22] Other suburbs will be left behind, unless they have good housing and attractive attributes. A majority of house-only suburbs, of whatever vintage, will struggle to attract new buyers. The mismatch of needs and resources will become a more pressing problem. Trickle-down processes will continue to reverse direction, with more preferences for old housing locations in most cities. In many suburbs, trickle-down processes will accelerate in their traditional path of decline as housing ages so that the virtues of new housing will be more fleeting.[23]

Local governance structure is ill-designed to cope with these conditions and trends. States have the capacity to restructure local governance. Some consolidation of governments can help. Some new partial metropolitan governance forms can help. More clarity in goals to reduce energy use can help. Innovations like mode neutrality, sustainability challenge contracts, and sustainable region incentive programs (discussed in Chapter 4), created by either federal or state governments or in the future by metropolitan governments, can help.

Ironically, the overarching problems of nonrenewable-resource depletion and climate change may eventually help us see more clearly the weaknesses of small units of local government. When metropolitan governance systems are reformed and redesigned, means of enhancing the basic capabilities of governance within metropolitan areas should be emphasized. Aspects of federal and state public-policy traditions can be drawn upon. Both individual responsibility and a shared responsibility approach to climate change are essential. Policies that enhance places and attract people are required. Markets must be structured more effectively. Federalism's relationships must be adjusted but cannot be rejected. The 21st-century American way of life also must change. Drawing on the historic tenacity of Americans who grappled with nature and tamed a continent has some virtues. But this time, reconstituting the bounty of nature will be the goal.

NOTES

1. Sylvie Tissot, "French Suburbs: A New Problem or a New Approach to Social Exclusion?" Center for European Studies Working Paper Series 160, 2008. Available at http://halshs.archives-ouvertes.fr/docs/00/28/50/25/PDF/CES_160-tissot-frenchSuburbs.pdf.
2. U.S. Bureau of Census, "2002 Census of Governments," Preliminary Report No. 1, Series GCO2-1(P), July 2002. Governing boards for these special districts were composed of representatives of cities and counties and sometimes smaller local governments. They rarely had directly elected members, although they assigned fees

for services provided, sometimes with approval of the local governments that they represented.

3. Ibid.

4. William H. Lucy and David L. Phillips, *Tomorrow's Cities, Tomorrow's Suburbs* (Chicago: APA Planners Press, 2006).

5. Robert Puentes and Linda Bailey, "Increasing Funding and Accountability for Metropolitan Transportation Decisions," in Bruce Katz and Robert Puentes, eds., *Taking the High Road: A Metropolitan Agenda for Transportation Reform* (Washington, D.C.: Brookings Institution, 2005), 151.

6. Eric M. Weiss, "In Va., Vision of Suburbia at a Crossroads," *Washington Post*, March 22, 2009.

7. Arthur C. Nelson and Robert E. Lang, *The New Politics of Planning* (Washington, D.C.: Urban Land Institute, 2009), 32, 33, 23, 19, and 28.

8. Rob Gurwitt, "The State vs. Sprawl," *Governing*, January 1999.

9. John M. DeGrove, *Planning Policy and Politics: Smart Growth and the States* (Cambridge, Mass.: Lincoln Institute of Land Policy, 2005), 277.

10. Lisa Rein, "Study Calls Md. Smart Growth a Flop," *Washington Post*, November 2, 2009.

11. Puentes and Bailey, "Increasing Funding and Accountability," 157.

12. Robert O. Self., "Prelude to the Tax Revolt: The Politics of the 'Tax Dollar' in Postwar California," in *The New Suburban History*, ed. Kevin M. Kruse and Thomas J. Sugrue (Chicago: University of Chicago Press, 2006).

13. Julia Lave Johnston and Kimberly Johnston-Dodds, "Common Interest Developments: Housing at Risk?" CRB Report 02-012 (Sacramento: California Research Bureau of the California State Library, 2002).

14. Harold Meyerson, "How the Golden State Got Tarnished," *Washington Post*, May 28, 2009.

15. Douglas Porter, *Managing Growth in America's Communities*, 2d ed. (Washington, D.C.: Island Press, 2008).

16. Myron Orfield, *Metropolitics* (Washington, D.C.: Brookings Institution, 1997).

17. David L. Phillips and William H. Lucy, "Suburban Decline Described and Interpreted, 1960 to 1990: 554 Suburbs in 24 Largest Urbanized Areas," report to the Center for Urban Development, Virginia Commonwealth University, Richmond, Va., 1996.

18. Marc Silver and William Mangino, "Looking Beyond the Classroom: The Impact of Economic and Racial Segregation on Student Achievement and Educational Outcomes," paper presented at *A Suburban World? Global Decentralization and the New Metropolis*, Reston, Va., April 7–8, 2008.

19. Ellen Dunham-Jones, *Retrofitting Suburbia* (New York: John Wiley, 2008).

20. Christopher Leinberger, "The Changing Location of Development and Investment Opportunities," *Urban Land* 45, no. 5 (1995): 31–36.

21. Ross Pulley, "MARC Home Loan Program Expands into Lee's Summit," *Kansas City Star*, March 13, 2009.

22. Robert Fishman, "The Fifth Migration," *Journal of the American Planning Association* 71, no. 4 (2005): 357–66.

23. Arthur C. Nelson, "Leadership in a New Era," *Journal of the American Planning Association* 72, no. 4 (2006): 393–407.

6

The Future of Politics

Global warming and oil depletion won't wait for metropolitan governance confusion to turn around. Federal and state governments will have to act. Changing the rules and incentives that affect local governments can help. Federal and state actions, however, must influence consumers in their role as home buyers and transportation users. They must influence developers' prospects for profits, and they must also support alternative energy sources.

Three types of federal action are needed. The first concerns taxes. The second concerns financing home buying. The third concerns energy.

TAXES

Gas-tax revenues that paid for constructing the 46,876-mile interstate highway system no longer are adequate to repair and replace what has been built. The gas tax has not been increased since 1993. It should be increased to pay for major highways and to help finance rail transit. Raising this tax will discourage the driving of gas guzzlers, increase use of efficient vehicles, and influence some people to live closer to work and other destinations.

An alternative would be to tax miles driven. The means of collecting this tax are not as simple as with a gas tax. And it is aimed more directly against the goal of buying a home in the suburbs or exurbs. This makes it tougher politically. Consequently, a gas tax seems preferable to a vehicle-miles-driven tax.

HOME BUYING

The years leading up to the 2008–2009 crises may be seen in retrospect as the last hurrah of the exurban extreme of the American dream. Cheap housing credit was propelling the drive for large houses on large lots to the edge of cornfields from 2000 to 2007. The eventual financial disasters were an outgrowth of deliberate public-policy goals to increase home ownership. The way in which public-policy goals intersected with lending and financial manipulations, and how these intersected with presidential and congressional politics, as explained in Chapter 1, is crucial to figuring out future public policies guiding home buying.

Three housing finance changes will be useful.

First, Fannie Mae and Freddie Mac should increase mortgage eligibility based on location-efficient mortgages, such as homes where people can drive short distances or have one car per household. Conversely, location-inefficient mortgages would include the cost of driving as part of the cost of being eligible for a mortgage. This would make it easier to buy in a central location and harder to buy in more remote locations.

Second, major remodeling mortgages would be expanded if Fannie Mae and Freddie Mac routinely purchased mortgages that seamlessly transitioned from construction loans to fixed-rate mortgages. In this way, buyers who remodel would avoid uncertainty as to whether they could get a mortgage at a reasonable rate after remodeling. This financing method for remodelers has been used successfully in the Chicago Historic Bungalow house expansion and energy upgrade program.[1] As down-payment requirements rise for long-term mortgages, seamless transitions from construction loans to fixed-rate mortgages will become more attractive, even necessary.

Third, deductions of mortgage interest and property taxes should be capped on owner-occupied dwellings. Since 1997, home owners can deduct up to $1 million in interest payments per year on a primary or second residence, rewarding wealthy owners and encouraging construction of large houses in sprawl settings.[2] Until 1998, owner-occupants paid capital-gains taxes if they did not buy an equal or more expensive replacement dwelling within two years of selling. This policy, now abandoned, encouraged sprawl development of large houses. Each of these policies would support closer-in development and redevelopment.

ENERGY

Although metropolitan governance is government's biggest shortcoming, when it comes to coping with global warming and oil depletion, interstate collaboration also is inadequate.

Some important activities in the decades to come will span several states. They include three key domains, which interact with private businesses: high-speed rail, electricity transmission lines from solar- and wind-energy farms, and cap-and-trade CO_2 systems with emphasis on coal-fired electric utilities.

Multistate regions and regulated private businesses are not organized into routinely functioning bureaucracies or standardized intergovernmental decision-making processes. Effective action depends on creating decision-making systems that do not fit well into standard operating procedures in current bureaucracies. Policy development and policy implementation are difficult. Every important subject is up for negotiation among state regulators and state governors who then must persuade state legislatures to pass legislation and fund projects.

High-speed rail will be concentrated in several corridors, with spurs extending from parts of the main routes.[3] Lines within a single state (examples include California, Florida, New York, and Texas) will be easier to finance and coordinate than multistate routes. Some states have adopted bond issues for high-speed rail, including approval of a $10 billion bond issue in California in 2008.[4]

The high-speed rail market is mainly for routes from 100 to 500 miles.[5] Within this range, high-speed rail would reduce travel times (compared with airlines) by shortening motor-vehicle connections from stations to specific destinations, cost travelers less per trip, and emit far less CO_2 because of the reduction in use of airplane fuel. It also would relieve interstate highway traffic, reducing maintenance and reconstruction costs.

But expanding high-speed rail will cost a lot. It requires train-track route straightening and upgrades, bridge capacity enhancements, and improvements at some crossings to make it safe. And of course, there are locomotives and passenger cars to order. Agreements and funding to build or improve entire multistate routes, or predictable paths by which such agreements can be forged, will enhance willingness of federal and state governments to plan, finance, and implement these projects.

Second, there is wind and solar power. The Great Plains states have been called the Saudi Arabia of wind-generated electric power, because winds are strong and frequent there. States in the Southwest have lots of sunlight for solar-generated electricity. But the strength of the electricity diminishes the farther it has to be transmitted over power lines. Some areas with the best wind- and solar-power potential are population centers, but the prime wind and solar areas often are low on water, limiting their future growth. Most Americans live far from prime wind and solar regions. They are clustered near coasts, around the Great Lakes, and near the Mississippi and Ohio rivers.

Installing additional electricity-transmission lines, therefore, is an important part of reducing our use of oil and coal and increasing the availability of renewable energy. It may be possible to improve transmission methods with changes in materials, but that is a research and development challenge. Transmission will require more lines and often new routes—a political as well as an economic challenge, because new routes always encounter opposition. The Federal Energy Regulatory Commission, which shares siting authority with state agencies, will need more authority over siting high-capacity transmission lines.[6]

Fitting these energy elements together profitably is unlikely without federal subsidies for research and development, federal intervention in state siting processes, and federal support to even out financial stresses that will arise if oil prices sometimes fall precipitously, as they did in the second half of 2008, or rise rapidly, as they did in the first half of 2008. Public financing, in particular for new transmission lines, may be needed. Federal policy habits and state regulatory policies are not integrated well to make these processes work smoothly or purposefully. Federal tax policies will be needed that encourage investment in renewable-energy generation and transmission.

Third, a cap-and-trade system to reduce CO_2 emissions will raise electricity rates in regions that depend on coal-fired electric power plants. In 2008, coal power plants generated 48 percent of U.S. electricity.[7] Midwest and Appalachian mountain states are more coal dependent for electricity than are other regions. Policies that temporarily limit the financial burden on consumers will be needed more in some regions than in others.[8]

If the Environmental Protection Agency administers new legislation, or if it acts under authority established in the Clean Air Act Amendments of 1990, it will be able to draw on its regulatory experience in implementing a cap-and-trade system for sulfur dioxide and other pollutants from power plants. That Clean Air Act policy was implemented by requiring smokestack technology that scrubs the most harmful chemicals, such as sulphur dioxide, from emissions. But no analogous technology exists for CO_2 emissions. New technology, if feasible, will be more expensive, such as carbon sequestration underground; substitute energy sources may be needed, which may be more costly to construct nearby (such as nuclear power) or to purchase from far away (such as wind or solar).

Regional subnationalism, for which no adequate models now exist, will need to create new approaches to each of these three subjects.

PROSPECTS

The most effective public policies influence behavior. Tax policies, if understood, do that. So the most effective policies relevant to climate change and oil depletion would raise the price of gasoline by taxing it more. But direct effects that are easily understood also encounter resistance.

Less direct but still effective policies involve finance. Mortgage finance, for example, through location-efficient and -inefficient mortgages will affect behavior, but it will not carry such a clear sense of being penalized as would higher taxes. Therefore, these policies and seamless transition financing from remodeling to long-term mortgages would be relatively easy to get approved politically.

Rewards for good conduct also tend to attract support, provided they do not clearly penalize others. Thus, sustainable region incentive programs or sustainability challenge contracts (Chapter 4) to support regional planning, action, and finance of public transportation are fairly promising candidates for political support.

Support for more money, such as channeling more funds into public transit, is the easiest policy to get approved, provided it is not clearly linked to some other attractive policy getting less funding.

With each of these policies, location-decision trends since 1990 have been gradually building voter support. Without these trends, proposals for each of these policy options probably would fail. But with these trends, as they accumulate, as they become better known, and as political agitation occurs, support for each of these policies will increase. This is the main reason why prospects for action on climate change and oil depletion are better than some think.

Other recent trends—more savings, less auto travel, fewer large vehicles purchased, and more transit use—add to longer-term trends that make a more compact, effective, and equitable metropolis more plausible.

In each case, we're seeing that people are changing behavior to cope with a changed economic reality. Some of the same people who were awash in self-centered excess one year, or one day, seem to have adopted recession- or even depression-based behavior overnight. As some changes in behavior occur, the potential for more changes increases, because behavior change signals attention to different information. The United States is an information-rich society. The news media will discover which messages consumers of information are noticing. Media in the Internet era are responsive and adaptive. So the pace of behavior change, now merely being hinted at, could become truly dramatic. Eventually, cars could return to their original role—a liberating opportunity but not a necessity.

NOTES

1. See www.chicagobungalows.org.
2. Alex F. Schwartz, *Housing Policy in the United States* (New York: Routledge, 2006).
3. Potential routes include Boston to New York City; New York City to Washington, D.C.; Washington, D.C. to Atlanta through Richmond, Raleigh, and Charlotte; Seattle to Eugene; Chicago to St. Louis and Milwaukee; Chicago to Cleveland; New York City to Buffalo; Dallas to San Antonio; Houston to New Orleans; Tampa and Miami to Orlando; and Fort Worth to Little Rock. Federal Railroad Administration, "High Speed Rail: Vision of High Speed Rail in America" (Washington, D.C.: U.S. Department of Transportation, 2009).
4. National Association of Railroad Passengers, "Hotline 578," November 7, 2008; available at www.narprail.org/cms/index.php/main/printable/hotline_578.
5. Lisa Stark and Kate Barrett, "President Obama to Lay Out Plans for High Speed Train Travel," ABCNews.com, April 12, 2009.
6. "Down to the Wire," editorial, *Washington Post*, April 10, 2009.
7. U.S. Energy Information Administration, "Net Generation by Energy Source" (2009), Table 1.1; available at www.eia.doe.gov/cneaf/electricity/epa/epat1p1.html.
8. Juliet Eilperin, "Science Chief Discusses Climate Strategy," *Washington Post*, April 9, 2009.

1

Demography
Is Destiny

HOUSING AND DEMOGRAPHICS

Were foreclosures in outer metropolitan counties influenced by less demand for large houses? Changes in the number of households in key home-buying cohorts from 2000 through 2008 are consistent with an interpretation that demand for large houses on large lots in remote metropolitan-area locations may be waning. Numbers of householders in age cohorts from 45 to 54, 55 to 64, and 65 and over expanded each year from 2000 through 2007. But the numbers of householders in the 30-to-34 group decreased in seven of these nine years, while the numbers in the 35-to-44 age cohort decreased in eight of nine years.[1] Home ownership rates increased most rapidly among householder cohorts aged 30 to 44. Home ownership in the 25-to-29 age group was 40.6 percent in 2007, jumping to 54.4 percent in ages 30 to 34 and to 67.8 percent in ages 35 to 44. Older groups had still higher home ownership rates: 75.4 to 80.6 percent.[2] These older groups will have more houses to sell as they retire, move, and downsize.

Examining age cohort trends before and after 2004 is instructive, because the home ownership rate peaked then at 69.2 percent. In 2004, the home ownership rate in the 25-to-29, 30-to-34, and 35-to-44-year age groups had increased from the 1994 to 2003 average. In 1994, the national home ownership rate was 64.0 percent. Ten years later, it had increased by 5.0 percent (and by 5.2 percent to the highest quarter in 2004). That 5 percent increase added 3.2 million more home owners, based on 63.5 million home owners in 1995.[3] That caused a tremendous boost to employment in housing construction, land development, real estate sales, building materials, home furnishing, mortgage initiation, and mortgage lending. Increases in prime home ownership age groups drove demand for housing. In the age groups from 35 to 54, when large increases occurred in first-time home buying and in move-up home transitions, an average of 793,000 more households existed each year in the United States from 1994 through 2003 (Table A.1). Thereafter, the rate of increase slowed in 2004 and 2005 through 2007 in the 45-to-54 age group.

In crucial younger age groups, 30 to 34 and 35 to 44, where the biggest increases in home ownership rates have occurred, the number of households decreased from 2004 to 2008. In 2008, there were 1.7 million fewer households headed by someone age 30 to 44 than in 2003. The average annual decrease was 184,000 for ages 30 to 34 and 226,000 for ages 35 to 44 during each of the four years from 2004 through 2007 when the home ownership rate declined to 68.1 percent in 2007 (Table A.1). Another decline of 100,000 occurred in the 35-to-44-year-old group in 2008. These ages also are prime periods for child rearing, with preferences increasing for larger residences and proximity to satisfactory schools. Reductions in demand for that type of housing in suburban locations may account for some of the high foreclosure rates in outlying counties in many metropolitan areas.

Another cause of high foreclosure rates may be the increase in home ownership that occurred in age groups in their 20s. These age groups had the biggest increase in home ownership rates of any age cohort during the 1995 to 2004 period.

TABLE A.1 AVERAGE HOME OWNERSHIP RATES AND AVERAGE ANNUAL NET CHANGE IN NUMBER OF HOUSEHOLDS BY AGE OF HOUSEHOLDER

PERCENTAGES	TOTAL	LESS THAN 25 YEARS	25 TO 29 YEARS	30 TO 34 YEARS	35 TO 44 YEARS	45 TO 54 YEARS	55 TO 64 YEARS	65 AND OVER
1994 to 2003	66.4	19.4	36.6	53.7	66.8	76.0	80.5	79.5
2004	69.0	25.2	40.2	57.4	69.2	77.2	81.7	81.1
2005 to 2007	68.6	25.1	41.1	55.7	68.7	76.1	80.9	80.6
2008	67.8	23.6	40.0	53.5	67.0	75.0	80.1	80.1
HOUSEHOLDS*								
1994 to 2003	1,347	120	−47	−71	193	600	369	182
2004	1,028	98	278	−219	−320	365	714	112
2005 to 2007	1,239	14	226	−172	−194	397	694	303
2008	1,103	−222	−75	−6	−100	293	697	517

*Units in Thousands

Source: U.S. Department of Housing and Urban Development, Tables 22 and 27: Housing Conditions in the United States; Historical Data, 2009.

These ages also are more mobile than older households. They are more likely to be making job changes, less likely to have children at home and in school, and more likely to move to other metropolitan areas. For householders of these ages, adjustable-rate mortgages (ARMs) that reset in two or more years are especially attractive, because many expect to move in two or three years. If housing prices continue to rise, as they did in most metropolitan areas until 2006, when single-family house prices peaked, then finding buyers and moving before ARMs reset to higher interest rates seemed smart.[4] In fact, if you didn't buy, it often seemed like a waste of a chance to make money. In markets with rapid price appreciation, California in particular, getting in on a good housing investment opportunity may have looked especially attractive, despite the risks that would accompany a downturn in prices—but a downturn had not occurred for a long time and must have seemed a remote prospect.

So the raw material to sustain demand for large single-unit houses in prime child-rearing areas was diminishing. With diminished numbers of replacement home buyers in the 30-to-44 age group, demand for large houses in outer metropolitan counties may diminish for demographic reasons and potentially for other reasons related to accessibility and travel costs. Locations of foreclosures and house value to family income ratios may foreshadow such transitions.

Potential for less demand for large suburban houses can be seen in other trends. As home ownership rates declined after 2004, the largest decline was in the 30-to-34 age category, which fell from 57.4 percent in 2004 to 52.2 percent in the fourth quarter of 2008.[5] In addition, the composition of married-couple households changed from 2003 through 2008. The number of husband-wife families with children declined by 523,000, an annual average of 87,000. Simultaneously, the number of husband-wife families without children at home increased by 1,993,000, an annual average of 332,000.[6] The result: fewer husband-wife families with children and fewer households in the prime years for buying four-bedroom houses.

THE ROLE OF INCOME

In eight of the metropolitan areas in the data set being used in this book, foreclosure data in central cities were available because the central cities also were counties. They displayed diverse patterns of foreclosure concentrations, but the central city usually had a lower foreclosure rate than one or several counties. This spatial pattern may reflect demand. In general, demand for owner-occupied housing may have been stronger in central cities relative to supply than in outer counties, resulting in lower foreclosure rates in cities. This outcome could occur because housing prices were less inflated relative to family incomes in these central cities.

But the opposite was more often the case. In San Francisco, for example, the median value of owner-occupied housing in 2007 was 9.7 times the median family income, yet the foreclosure rate was a mere 0.24 percent. In the District of Columbia, housing values were 6.8 times family income, yet the foreclosure rate was 0.12 percent. And in New York City, housing values were 12.3 times family income in Brooklyn (foreclosure rate 0.38), 11.7 times family income in Manhattan (foreclosure rate 0.04 percent), and 10.3 times family income in the Bronx (foreclosure rate 0.28 percent). Other central cities lacked such extraordinary house value–to-income ratios, but in no instance were low foreclosure rates associated with low house value–to-income ratios (Table A.2).

Perhaps city residents' income capacity was not represented well by median family income. With lower owner-occupancy rates in central cities (54 percent) compared with suburbs (76 percent), more home owners in cities may be relatively high on the income scale rather than near the median income.[7] In addition, if demand for city home ownership was high relative to ownership opportunities, people who got in financial trouble paying mortgages may have been able to sell at prices high enough to pay their mortgage holder in full. This prospect was one motivator for the housing bubble—the prospect of being able to sell and make a profit even if household income and ability to pay the mortgage diminished. Perhaps selling at a

TABLE A.2 HOUSE VALUES, FAMILY INCOME, AND FORECLOSURES IN CENTRAL CITIES

Central City Counties	2007 Ratio of Median Owner-Occupied Housing Value to Median Family Income	2008 Foreclosures to Housing Units (%)
Baltimore	3.5	0.16
Denver	4.3	2.23
Philadelphia	3.0	0.53
San Francisco	9.7	0.24
St. Louis	3.0	1.02
Norfolk	4.2	0.19
Washington, D.C.	6.8	0.12
New York	—	—
Brooklyn (Kings)	12.3	0.38
Bronx	10.3	0.28
Manhattan (New York)	11.7	0.04
Queens	8.4	0.51
Staten Island (Richmond)	6.0	0.77
12 Central City County Average	6.9	0.12
7 Central City County Average without New York	4.9	0.64
U.S. National Average	3.2	0.79

Sources: foreclosure.com, U.S. Bureau of the Census, American Community Survey 2007

Note: These central cities are counties or central cities that contain several counties (e.g., New York City contains five counties). Other central cities are parts of counties that also contain suburbs.

profit persisted longer and more frequently in these central cities than in suburban counties.

A useful indicator of vulnerability to mortgage-payment delinquencies and foreclosures is the percentage of household income that mortgage holders paid for housing costs. Sheila Bair, chair of the Federal Deposit Insurance Corporation (FDIC), advocated and implemented a mortgage-adjustment plan in which owner-occupants would pay 31 percent of income for mortgage-related costs. Traditional lenders and Fannie Mae have required about 30 percent, depending on various factors, of gross income paid for mortgage-related costs. Yet, in 2007, 13.6 percent of mortgage holders reported that they spent more than 50 percent of household income on housing costs, up from 9.0 percent in 2000. In high housing-cost jurisdictions, such as those in the Los Angeles metropolitan area, more than 20 percent of mortgage holders were paying more than 50 percent of income for housing costs in 2007.[8]

The ratio of median value of owner-occupied housing to median family income increased from 2.4 in 2000 to 3.2 in 2007. This increase was strongly influenced by the 12 states above 4.0 in 2007, led by California at housing values 8.3 times family incomes. The average increase of these 12 states was 73 percent between 2000 and 2007. In 2007, 16 states still were at housing values 2.4 or less times family income. The average increase in these 16 states between 2000 and 2007 was 12 percent. High house values and high increases in house values relative to family income were creating financial imbalances in some states. These imbalances were raw material from which foreclosures could be forged if the housing bubble burst or if recession occurred. When excessive risk stretched borrowers to the breaking point, reductions in earnings, however brief, made many owners delinquent in mortgage payments. When house prices fell below the value of mortgages, which sometimes lacked down payments and owner equity, sales brought additional losses to sellers. Lower values and lower earnings led to a rapid increase in foreclosure proceedings.

One benefit of foreclosures concentrated in a few states was that price declines rapidly reduced the house value–to-income imbalances that fed the foreclosure crisis. Housing in these high-price markets was becoming more affordable. The National Association of Realtors compiles an existing single-family affordability index that includes median prices and median family income. It showed a 2007 affordability index value of 111.8 followed by a 2008 index value of 128.6, with a 2008 fourth-quarter affordability index value for first-time home buyers of 146.5, a considerable improvement.[9] If maintained, the 2008 affordability index would show housing affordable to more families than in any year since 2003. The affordability index was influenced by mortgage interest rates, but mortgage rates were lower in 2003 than in 2008.[10]

When housing prices decline, affordability increases. It could improve the long-term growth prospects for states with excessive housing prices, if those prices approach the national average. If Richard Florida is correct that skilled employees are the knowledge-based private sector's most important element of production, then affordable housing prices are an inducement to positive growth and excessive prices impede economic development. High-tech Silicon Valley industries in California have understood this relationship for many years and have made affordable housing subsidies for employees a priority.[11] Realigning house prices toward a goal of three times family income will enhance the competitiveness of knowledge-based businesses in high-housing-price states.

PRICING "TOXIC MORTGAGE ASSETS"

An obstacle to formulating remedies for the national financial crisis that followed the foreclosure crisis was difficulty in pricing and accessing so-called toxic assets. Assets are referred to as toxic if they are worth substantially less than their original valuations by lenders or buyers of repackaged mortgages. As mortgages were purchased from lenders and bundled in into mortgage-backed securities (MBSs), which are various forms of securities paying a given interest rate, mortgages were separated from the original lender and reallocated in forms that were difficult to disentangle. MBSs limited the ability of mortgage servicers to renegotiate mortgage terms with delinquent home owners at risk of foreclosure and repossession. Lacking a market, many bundled MBSs had undetermined values. If valued at zero or some small fraction of their original value, these assets were toxic in the sense that they weighed heavily against the reserves banks are required to maintain against liabilities.

The absence of a market blocked the federal government from establishing a value for many MBSs backed by delinquent and foreclosed mortgages. But an estimate of the cost of buying these mortgages, if they can be separated from MBSs, was possible. Data in this study for housing values relative to family income could be used.

Like lenders of origin, Fannie Mae, Freddie Mac, and the FDIC have required that monthly housing costs approximate 30 percent of gross monthly income. The relationship between housing values and family income can be used to calculate how much prices should decline to rebalance house values and income, while returning foreclosure rates to traditional levels. With 62 percent of foreclosures occurring in California, Florida, Nevada, and Arizona, price declines to rebalance housing prices and income can be calculated. Returning California to the 4.0-to-1 ratio of housing values to family income in 2000 would cut the 2007 median value of owner-occupied housing ($535,700) to $258,252 (four times median family income of $64,563). That would be a price reduction in California of $277,448 per foreclosed house, a cut of 51.8 percent. To accomplish a reduction to the 2007 national average, when housing values were 3.2 times family income, Florida prices would fall 24.4 percent, Nevada's by 37.6 percent, and Arizona's by 24.6 percent.

If all the listed 2008 foreclosures and preforeclosures became repossessions, then these value reductions would cost $95 billion in California, $10 billion in Florida, $5 billion in Nevada, and $4 billion in Arizona—a total of $114 billion. This estimate overstated the crisis dimension of foreclosures. From 1997 through 2006, the average foreclosure rate was 0.42 percent of mortgage loans, about one-third of the 2008 rate.[12] It had become the normal cost of being in the mortgage business. Consequently, the foreclosure crisis should be considered, at most, the number and rate of foreclosures above the previous decade's norm.

An extreme perspective on pricing mortgage-backed toxic assets can be acquired by projecting 2008 foreclosure losses if housing prices decline to the ratios of housing values to family income in 2000. Calculating declines in the 34 states above the 2000 national ratio of house values to family incomes (2.4) in 2007, the loss from lower house values would be about $143 billion. In all

50 states, the decline to 2000 house values would be about $145 billion, with 87 percent in four states—California $95 billion (66 percent), Florida $18 billion (13 percent), Nevada $6.5 billion (5 percent), and Arizona $5.5 billion (4 percent). Declines of $1 billion or more also would occur in Illinois, New Jersey, New York, Massachusetts, Colorado, and Washington.

Eight of the 12 states with house value–to–family income ratios above 4.0 had low foreclosure rates—Hawaii, Massachusetts, New York, New Jersey, Rhode Island, Maryland, Oregon, and Washington (see Appendix 2). Consequently, the example above based on returning house value–to–family income ratios in 2000 exaggerates potential toxic-asset losses in most states.

HOW TO COUNTER A "BUBBLE"?

Rapid increases in housing prices driven by speculation and rapid price decreases driven by foreclosures and less demand are difficult to interpret. Diverse causes and motivations exist. Some speculators buy houses with the intention of "flipping" them by selling them for higher prices without ever occupying them. Some owner-occupants buy in hopes that their incomes will rise by the time higher interest rates kick in on their ARMs. Some owner-occupants buy in fear that their hope of buying a house will become more remote with each passing year as prices rise. Some owners do not understand the extent to which higher interest rates in their ARMs will become difficult to afford. And some price increases are driven by easy credit, increasing competition for the houses for sale, creating an impression that supply lags behind demand when demand may be artificially stimulated by easy credit, fear, and speculation. When demand slackens, supply turns out to be excessive rather than insufficient. Then price declines are fueled by oversupply as well as by foreclosures.

A few states, mainly Nevada, California, Arizona, and Florida, have been engulfed in this boom-and-bust rhythm. The boom carried these states into unsustainable relationships between house values and family income. Rebalancing house values and income required prices to fall. Lenders had a choice. They could foreclose and resell at drastically lower prices, or they could negotiate extended terms—a longer mortgage and delinquency forgiveness—that would limit but not avoid short-term losses. Until housing supply came down to lower levels (the national supply exceeded 10 months, with longer supply chains in some states, in 2008), house prices would not stabilize.

Because foreclosures typically lead to lower resale prices, and because foreclosure processes cost lenders money, lenders seem to have an interest in writing down principal in some instances to keep owners in their homes and to avoid foreclosure costs. If lenders had accurate information about which owners will default rather than recover from being delinquent in payments, and they could obtain that information inexpensively, more renegotiated terms, including principal writedowns, would occur. But Kristopher Gerardi and Paul Willen explain that lenders who make mistaken guesses about who will default face larger losses per loan than if they refuse to reduce principal.[13] Lenders also avoid establishing a reputation for writing down principal that may invite more such requests.

In California, in particular, house values grew to such unreasonable multiples of family income (more than eight times incomes in 2007) that writedowns through foreclosures of more than $200,000 were needed merely to return to the high-cost conditions of 2000, when house values were four times family incomes. For traditional lending practices to work, with down payments, fixed-rate mortgages, and incomes verified to be in the range of 30 percent of monthly mortgage costs, very large reductions in house prices became necessary. These price reductions can become positive influences on housing affordability and economic development, after the shock of absorbing large writedowns works through the financial systems.

In 2007, California had only 10.4 percent of the housing units in the United States. In 2008, that state had 33.9 percent of the foreclosures in the United States. If housing values relative to median family income were to fall to 2000 ratios of housing values to family income, California would account for 65.6 percent of the reduction in housing values. Moreover, California provided warnings in census data about looming crisis conditions; the American Community Survey revealed that the ratio of median value of owner-occupied housing to median family income increased from 4.0 in 2000 to 6.7 in 2004, 7.8 in 2005, and 8.3 in 2006, with a three-year average, from 2005 to 2007, of 8.3.

If national trends (such as national home-ownership policies and national tendencies such as private lenders seeking front-end mortgage initiation fees and the prevalence of other fees and interest-rate swaps that provided banks and insurance companies with large short-term profits) caused the foreclosure crisis and the ensuing financial crisis, what caused the house value–to–income imbalances that fueled these crises to be concentrated in California? And why were so many willing participants in escalating the housing bubble playing their games in California? Was something "Californian" going on, or was California merely an unlucky victim? Does California embody conditions that could lead to a new housing bubble?

The answers aren't certain, but it doesn't hurt to speculate. The huge run-up in housing prices in California created opportunities for large gains for home buyers if price increases continued. Thus, more households may have been attracted to potential gains—worried, perhaps, that they would be priced out of the home buying market if they did not act quickly.[14] A higher proportion of householders in the 25-to-34 age range became home owners by 2007 rather than renters. Some lenders (such as Countrywide) specializing in subprime, no-principal, interest-only loans, with no income checks, got their starts in California and focused there. Expansion of prime home buying age groups up to 2000 was followed by a decline in these groups in California. From 2000 to 2007, ages 45 to 64 increased by 709,616, while ages 25 to 44 declined by 105,645.[15]

Perhaps public policies had some effects. An example might be the hindering of infill construction and transit-oriented development in the city of San Francisco and other attractive cities and inner suburbs. And perhaps Proposition 13 was influential. Because Proposition 13 limited property-tax increases to 2 percent per year, home buyers could buy with a low-interest ARM, perhaps interest only, for two or more years, pay little more in property taxes in the second and third years as their property value increased, and sell at a substantial profit in two or three years before the higher, reset ARM interest rate became too burdensome—an attractive opportunity for some young buyers anticipating moving. More than three in four home owners age 21 to 34 in California moved within five years. Whatever the causes, extra-high house value–to–family income ratios in California made it harder to push back against the foreclosure crisis.

To return stability to housing finance and to return to a reliable rate of housing construction and resale of existing dwellings, sustainable home ownership levels are required. Lending manipulations that drove the home-ownership rate to 69 percent were not sustainable. The 65 percent home ownership rate lasted for a long time, suggesting that it was sustainable. Whether it can or should be higher than 65 percent is an important policy question. As the distribution of income has become more skewed, and with the recession deepening, retaining a 65 percent home ownership rate may be difficult.

DATA SOURCES AND ISSUES

Counting Foreclosures

Foreclosure data are difficult to compare from one source to another. The "foreclosure" label may include delinquency notices, formal filings of intent to foreclose, repossessions through foreclosure processes, and property sales via sheriffs' auctions. These processes may be interrupted by delinquencies being paid, changes in lenders' enforcement policies, or legislation requiring delays in foreclosure proceedings. The same property may be listed multiple times.[16]

Up-to-date sources, like RealtyTrac.com and foreclosure .com, aim their services at potential buyers of foreclosed properties. RealtyTrac's data for foreclosure proceedings (2.3 million) more than doubled the foreclosure rate of foreclosure.com in 2008. But RealtyTrac reported "more than 860,000 properties were actually repossessed by lenders" in 2008—37 percent of foreclosure proceedings.[17] Foreclosure.com's website said, "home foreclosures jumped 64% to nearly one million homes in 2008." In our study, we used foreclosure.com data for states and counties, usually from November 2008. The U.S. number of foreclosures and preforeclosures in that source was 1,009,485.

The U.S. Department of Housing and Urban Development (HUD) has reported that repossession data were not available from the American Mortgage Bankers Association, so HUD developed a method of estimating repossessions from other data. Charles Capone estimated that 55 to 59 percent of formal foreclosure filings resulted in repossession of single-unit residential properties from their owners in the 1980s and 1990s.[18] The HUD study by Capone was in response to concern in Congress that the foreclosure rate was excessive.[19] Consequently, the foreclosure crisis of 2007 and 2008 was an increase from a substantial level of foreclosures that had become common. The RealtyTrac repossession rate of 37 percent (860,000 repossessions of 2.3 million foreclosure filings) in 2008 is far below the repossession rate of 55 to 59 percent estimated by Capone using 1990s data.

Different data comparisons can yield different impressions. Here we compare foreclosures to housing units to arrive at a foreclosure rate. Comparing foreclosures to mortgages is more common and yields a higher rate as well as leaves out owner-occupied housing where mortgages have been paid completely (32 percent of owner-occupied dwellings). This method also diminishes the importance of rental housing (32 percent of housing nationwide and 46 percent of housing in central cities) on which there are fewer foreclosures. By comparing foreclosures to housing units, we include all housing. This measure, however, understates the burden of delinquent mortgage payments on lenders. With 51 million mortgages in 2007, one million foreclosures would be 2 percent of all mortgages, five times more than the previous norm of 0.4 percent of mortgages starting the foreclosure process from 1997 to 2006.

Measuring Income

We use median family income rather than median household income data. Although most news coverage relies on household income, there is a gap between what the word "household" evokes in a reader's mind and what it really means to the Census. A "household" can be a single person or a group of unrelated roommates. Most single-unit detached residences—which means most owner-occupied housing mortgages—are occupied by families.

Median family income is higher: 19 percent higher in 2000 ($50,046 versus $41,994 for median household income). That alters the ratio of income to housing value. A considerably higher percentage of married-couple families own their residences than do nonfamily households: in 2000, for example, it was more than 80 percent for the former, while in 2007 it was just 53 percent for the latter.[20]

NOTES

1. U.S. Department of Housing and Urban Development (HUD), *U.S. Housing Market Conditions: Historical Data* (Washington, D.C., 2009), Table 22.
2. U.S. HUD, *U.S. Housing Market Conditions: Historical Data* (Washington, D.C., 2008), Table 27.
3. Ibid., Table 25.
4. Ibid., Table 9.
5. U.S. HUD, *U.S. Housing Market Conditions* (2009), Table 27.
6. Ibid., Table 23.
7. U.S. HUD, *U.S. Housing Market Conditions* (2008), Table 28.
8. U.S. Bureau of the Census, "American Community Survey, Census of Population and Housing, 2005–2007" (2008), Detailed Tables, Table B25091.
9. National Association of Realtors, "Housing Affordability Index and First-Time Homebuyer Affordability" (2009); available at www.realtor.org/research/research/housinginx. See also U.S. HUD, *U.S. Housing Market Conditions* (2009), Table 11.
10. U.S. HUD, *U.S. Housing Market Conditions* (2008), Table 11.
11. Silicon Valley Leadership Group, "Mission, Vision, and History," January 29, 2009; available at https://svlg.net/about/mission.php.
12. U.S. HUD, *U.S. Housing Market Conditions* (2008), 73.
13. Kristopher S. Gerardi and Paul S. Willen, "Subprime Mortgages, Foreclosures, and Urban Neighborhoods," Federal Reserve Bank of Boston Public Policy Discussion Papers, December 22, 2008, 20–21.

14. Dowell Myers and SungHo Ryu, "Aging Baby Boomers and the Generational Housing Bubble," *Journal of the American Planning Association* 74, no. 1 (2008): 17–33.
15. U.S. Bureau of the Census, "Census of Population and Housing 2000" (2003), American Factfinder, Detailed Tables; and U.S. Bureau of the Census, "American Community Survey, Census of Population and Housing, 2005–2007," Table B25091.
16. Diana Olick, "RealtyTrac: Real Numbers or Hype?" CNBC.com, June 13, 2007.
17. Associated Press, "Foreclosures Increased 81 Percent Last Year," January 15, 2009.
18. Charles A. Capone Jr., "Providing Alternatives to Mortgage Foreclosure: A Report to Congress" (Washington, D.C.: U.S. HUD, 1996).
19. Ibid.
20. U.S. HUD, *U.S. Housing Market Conditions* (2008), 85.

Foreclosures, Housing Units, Housing Values, and Family Incomes

Data for foreclosures and preforeclosures, occupied housing units, median value of owner-occupied housing, median family income, and ratios between these indicators are reported here for 236 counties in the 35 most populous metropolitan statistical areas (MSAs). The sum of foreclosures and preforeclosures is compared to the number of occupied housing units. This comparison to housing units includes rented units, which have had a lower foreclosure rate than owner-occupied units. This comparison is a useful indicator of housing conditions, including supply-and-demand relationships. It does not capture the vulnerability of financial institutions. For that purpose, comparing the number of foreclosures to the number of mortgages would be more instructive.

In 2007, data for counties with low populations were not available for the number of housing units, housing values, and median family incomes. In these instances, the counties are included in the tables with data for the number of foreclosures and preforeclosures.

ATLANTA MSA HOUSING VALUE, FAMILY INCOME, AND FORECLOSURES

	2008 FORECLOSURES AND PREFORECLOSURES	2007 HOUSING UNITS	NUMBER OF HOUSING UNITS TO FORECLOSURES AND PREFORECLOSURES
United States	1,009,485	127,895,430	127
Georgia	22,837	3,961,643	173
Counties			
Barrow	288	24,813	86
Bartow	195	37,013	190
Butts	86		
Carroll	356	45,392	128
Cherokee	451	78,912	175
Clayton	1,471	105,986	72
Cobb	1,422	278,096	196
Coweta	270	45,989	170
Dawson	61		
Dekalb	3091	306,133	99
Douglas	509	48,509	95
Fayette	187	38,955	208
Forsyth	165	60,155	365
Fulton	5,233	431,617	82
Gwinnett	2,233	283,711	127
Haralson	51		
Heard	24		
Henry	891	71,270	80
Jasper	39		
Lamar	34		
Meriwether	27		
Newton	535	36,969	69
Paulding	407	50,308	124
Pickens	40		
Pike	28		
Rockdale	352	31,165	89
Spalding	152		
Walton	391	31,814	81

NOTE:
County foreclosure data from foreclosure.com on 11/7/2008.
State foreclosure data from foreclosure.com on 10/20/2008.
Income and housing data from census.gov 2007 American Community Survey.
No data were available for blank cells.

% OF HOUSING UNITS UNDER FORECLOSURE OR PREFORECLOSURE	2007 MEDIAN VALUE OF OWNER-OCCUPIED HOUSING	2007 MEDIAN FAMILY INCOME	RATIO OF HOUSING VALUE TO MEDIAN FAMILY INCOME
0.79	$185,200	$58,526	3.2
0.58	$156,800	$56,112	2.8
1.16	$142,700	$53,682	2.7
0.53	$155,100	$54,141	2.9
0.78	$138,800	$60,500	2.3
0.57	$204,400	$67,698	3.0
1.39	$132,000	$46,919	2.8
0.51	$219,800	$79,877	2.8
0.59	$178,900	$62,577	2.9
1.01	$197,700	$61,911	3.2
1.05	$160,300	$60,718	2.6
0.48	$254,700	$88,447	2.9
0.27	$284,400	$91,898	3.1
1.21	$267,800	$82,508	3.2
0.79	$201,800	$72,772	2.8
1.25	$177,800	$68,945	2.6
1.45	$149,400	$52,721	2.8
0.81	$146,900	$63,312	2.3
1.13	$189,600	$69,442	2.7
1.23	$159,300	$54,108	2.9

BALTIMORE MSA HOUSING VALUE, FAMILY INCOME, AND FORECLOSURES

	2008 FORECLOSURES AND PREFORECLOSURES	2007 HOUSING UNITS	NUMBER OF HOUSING UNITS TO FORECLOSURES AND PREFORECLOSURES
United States	1,009,485	127,895,430	127
Maryland	3,312	2,318,430	700
Counties			
Baltimore City	478	294,732	617
Baltimore	205	327,566	1,598
Anne Arundel	186	202,712	1,090
Carroll	46	61,433	1,336
Hartford	92	95,824	1,042
Howard	80	104,216	1,303
Queen Anne's	22		

NOTE:
County foreclosure data from foreclosure.com on 10/23/2008.
State foreclosure data from foreclosure.com on 10/17/08.
Income and housing data from census.gov 2007 American Community Survey.
No data were available for blank cells.

BOSTON MSA HOUSING VALUE, FAMILY INCOME, AND FORECLOSURES

	2008 FORECLOSURES AND PREFORECLOSURES	2007 HOUSING UNITS	NUMBER OF HOUSING UNITS TO FORECLOSURES AND PREFORECLOSURES
United States	1,009,485	127,895,430	127
Massachusetts	7,861	2,722,323	346
Counties			
Essex	1,166	297,471	255
Middlesex	1,357	593,246	437
Norfolk	513	265,055	517
Plymouth	843	192,637	229
Rockingham, N.H.	219	123,556	564
Strafford, N.H.	107	50,230	469
Suffolk	1,086	298,906	275

NOTE:
County foreclosure data from foreclosure.com on 11/9/2008.
State foreclosure data from foreclosure.com on 10/20/2008.
Income and housing data from census.gov 2007 American Community Survey.

% OF HOUSING UNITS UNDER FORECLOSURE OR PREFORECLOSURE	2007 MEDIAN VALUE OF OWNER-OCCUPIED HOUSING	2007 MEDIAN FAMILY INCOME	RATIO OF HOUSING VALUE TO MEDIAN FAMILY INCOME
0.79	$185,200	$58,526	3.2
0.14	$334,700	$77,839	4.3
0.16	$158,400	$45,353	3.5
0.06	$273,000	$76,951	3.5
0.09	$384,200	$92,100	4.2
0.07	$371,400	$95,146	3.9
0.10	$307,500	$83,443	3.7
0.08	$478,500	$115,707	4.1

% OF HOUSING UNITS UNDER FORECLOSURE OR PREFORECLOSURE	2007 MEDIAN VALUE OF OWNER-OCCUPIED HOUSING	2007 MEDIAN FAMILY INCOME	RATIO OF HOUSING VALUE TO MEDIAN FAMILY INCOME
0.79	$185,200	$58,526	3.2
0.29	$370,400	$74,463	5.0
0.39	$385,900	$80,103	4.8
0.23	$441,400	$93,997	4.7
0.19	$421,000	$99,740	4.2
0.44	$375,300	$82,458	4.6
0.18	$326,900	$89,939	3.6
0.21	$230,900	$72,023	3.2
0.36	$410,000	$56,106	7.3

BUFFALO MSA HOUSING VALUE, FAMILY INCOME, AND FORECLOSURES

	2008 FORECLOSURES AND PREFORECLOSURES	2007 HOUSING UNITS	NUMBER OF HOUSING UNITS TO FORECLOSURES AND PREFORECLOSURES
United States	1,009,485	127,895,430	127
New York	13,198	7,940,072	602
Counties			
Erie	323	422,880	1,309
Niagara	75	97,943	1,306

NOTE:
County foreclosure data from foreclosure.com on 10/27/2008.
State foreclosure data from foreclosure.com on 10/16/2008.
Income and housing data from census.gov 2007 American Community Survey.

CHARLOTTE MSA HOUSING VALUE, FAMILY INCOME, AND FORECLOSURES

	2008 FORECLOSURES AND PREFORECLOSURES	2007 HOUSING UNITS	NUMBER OF HOUSING UNITS TO FORECLOSURES AND PREFORECLOSURES
United States	1,009,485	127,895,430	127
North Carolina	5,432	4,124,066	759
Counties			
Anson	15	10,499	700
Cabarrus	207	65,005	314
Gaston	231	85,967	372
Mecklenburg	1,231	374,536	304
Union	240	63,683	265
York, S.C.	161	82,856	515

NOTE:
County foreclosure data from foreclosure.com on 11/7/2008.
State foreclosure data from foreclosure.com on 10/20/2008.
Income and housing data from census.gov 2007 American Community Survey.

% OF HOUSING UNITS UNDER FORECLOSURE OR PREFORECLOSURE	2007 MEDIAN VALUE OF OWNER-OCCUPIED HOUSING	2007 MEDIAN FAMILY INCOME	RATIO OF HOUSING VALUE TO MEDIAN FAMILY INCOME
0.79	$185,200	$58,526	3.2
0.17	$303,400	$62,138	4.9
0.08	$112,000	$60,630	1.8
0.08	$95,800	$58,152	1.6

% OF HOUSING UNITS UNDER FORECLOSURE OR PREFORECLOSURE	2007 MEDIAN VALUE OF OWNER-OCCUPIED HOUSING	2007 MEDIAN FAMILY INCOME	RATIO OF HOUSING VALUE TO MEDIAN FAMILY INCOME
0.79	$185,200	$58,526	3.2
0.13	$137,200	$52,336	2.6
0.14	$79,900	$36,611	2.2
0.32	$145,800	$61,404	2.4
0.27	$111,800	$51,432	2.2
0.33	$173,900	$64,655	2.7
0.38	$172,800	$57,485	3.0
0.19	$147,100	$62,144	2.4

CHICAGO MSA HOUSING VALUE, FAMILY INCOME, AND FORECLOSURES

	2008 FORECLOSURES AND PREFORECLOSURES	2007 HOUSING UNITS	NUMBER OF HOUSING UNITS TO FORECLOSURES AND PREFORECLOSURES
United States	1,009,485	127,895,430	127
Illinois	84,523	5,246,116	62
Counties			
Cook	43,463	2,172,770	50
Dekalb	528	38,684	73
DuPage	5,448	358,720	66
Grundy	235		
Kane	3,860	172,160	45
Kendall	874	33,394	38
Kenosha, Wisc.	96	67,430	702
Lake, Ill.	4,975	252,685	51
Lake, Ind.	544	209,347	385
McHenry	2,279	114,508	50
Newton, Ind.	6		
Porter, Ind.	52	65,523	1,260
Will	5,266	229,590	44

NOTE:
County foreclosure data from foreclosure.com on 10/25/2008.
State foreclosure data from foreclosure.com on 10/16/2008.
Income and housing data from census.gov 2007 American Community Survey.
No data were available for blank cells.

% OF HOUSING UNITS UNDER FORECLOSURE OR PREFORECLOSURE	2007 MEDIAN VALUE OF OWNER-OCCUPIED HOUSING	2007 MEDIAN FAMILY INCOME	RATIO OF HOUSING VALUE TO MEDIAN FAMILY INCOME
0.79	$185,200	$58,526	3.2
1.61	$200,200	$63,121	3.2
2.00	$281,800	$63,204	4.5
1.36	$205,000	$72,006	2.8
1.52	$325,400	$89,098	3.7
2.24	$250,600	$77,050	3.3
2.62	$249,300	$82,144	3.0
0.14	$187,500	$68,659	2.7
1.97	$310,700	$89,257	3.5
0.26	$136,300	$57,389	2.4
1.99	$262,100	$83,186	3.2
0.08	$163,300	$71,292	2.3
2.29	$243,900	$80,997	3.0

CINCINNATI MSA HOUSING VALUE, FAMILY INCOME, AND FORECLOSURES

	2008 FORECLOSURES AND PREFORECLOSURES	2007 HOUSING UNITS	NUMBER OF HOUSING UNITS TO FORECLOSURES AND PREFORECLOSURES
United States	1,009,485	127,895,430	127
Ohio	14,848	5,065,254	341
Counties			
Boone, Ky.	72	44,194	614
Bracken, Ky.	2		
Brown	49		
Butler	415	143,674	346
Campbell, Ky.	111	38,899	350
Clermont	124	77,809	627
Dearborn, Ind.	23		
Franklin, Ind.	7		
Gallatin, Ky.	8		
Grant, Ky.	20		
Hamilton	1,020	384,257	377
Kenton, Ky.	127	70,336	554
Ohio, Ind.	6		
Pendleton, Ky.	10		
Warren	230	75,922	330

NOTE:
County foreclosure data from foreclosure.com on 11/10/2008.
State foreclosure data from foreclosure.com on 10/16/2008.
Income and housing data from census.gov 2007 American Community Survey.
No data were available for blank cells.

% OF HOUSING UNITS UNDER FORECLOSURE OR PREFORECLOSURE	2007 MEDIAN VALUE OF OWNER-OCCUPIED HOUSING	2007 MEDIAN FAMILY INCOME	RATIO OF HOUSING VALUE TO MEDIAN FAMILY INCOME
0.79	$185,200	$58,526	3.2
0.29	$135,200	$56,148	2.4
0.16	$176,600	$77,422	2.3
0.29	$164,000	$67,069	2.4
0.29	$137,400	$68,434	2.0
0.16	$162,000	$64,194	2.5
0.27	$148,200	$64,019	2.3
0.18	$147,900	$64,020	2.3
0.30	$200,900	$81,773	2.5

CLEVELAND MSA HOUSING VALUE, FAMILY INCOME, AND FORECLOSURES

	2008 FORECLOSURES AND PREFORECLOSURES	2007 HOUSING UNITS	NUMBER OF HOUSING UNITS TO FORECLOSURES AND PREFORECLOSURES
United States	1,009,485	127,895,430	127
Ohio	14,848	5,065,254	341
Counties			
Cuyahoga	3,265	620,991	190
Geauga	41	35,435	864
Lake	260	98,727	380
Lorain	320	122,885	384
Medina	59	66,229	1,123

NOTE:
County foreclosure data from foreclosure.com on 11/9/2008.
State foreclosure data from foreclosure.com on 10/16/2008.
Income and housing data from census.gov 2007 American Community Survey.

COLUMBUS MSA HOUSING VALUE, FAMILY INCOME, AND FORECLOSURES

	2008 FORECLOSURES AND PREFORECLOSURES	2007 HOUSING UNITS	NUMBER OF HOUSING UNITS TO FORECLOSURES AND PREFORECLOSURES
United States	1,009,485	127,895,430	127
Ohio	14,848	5,065,254	341
Counties			
Delaware	106	60,014	566
Fairfield	164	55,377	338
Franklin	3,686	517,830	140
Licking	186	65,228	351
Madison	33	15,388	466
Morrow	11	13,022	1,184
Pickaway	50	19,723	394
Union	31	18,374	593

NOTE:
County foreclosure data from foreclosure.com on 11/10/2008.
State foreclosure data from foreclosure.com on 10/16/2008.
Income and housing data from census.gov 2007 American Community Survey.

% OF HOUSING UNITS UNDER FORECLOSURE OR PREFORECLOSURE	2007 MEDIAN VALUE OF OWNER-OCCUPIED HOUSING	2007 MEDIAN FAMILY INCOME	RATIO OF HOUSING VALUE TO MEDIAN FAMILY INCOME
0.79	$185,200	$58,526	3.2
0.29	$135,200	$56,148	2.4
0.53	$142,000	$57,463	2.5
0.12	$234,000	$79,053	3.0
0.26	$156,100	$66,140	2.4
0.26	$147,900	$58,973	2.5
0.09	$184,900	$70,727	2.6

% OF HOUSING UNITS UNDER FORECLOSURE OR PREFORECLOSURE	2007 MEDIAN VALUE OF OWNER-OCCUPIED HOUSING	2007 MEDIAN FAMILY INCOME	RATIO OF HOUSING VALUE TO MEDIAN FAMILY INCOME
0.79	$185,200	$58,526	3.2
0.29	$135,200	$56,148	2.4
0.18	$246,600	$94,099	2.6
0.30	$167,100	$66,225	2.5
0.71	$154,600	$60,953	2.5
0.29	$149,600	$63,871	2.3
0.21	$142,300	$63,959	2.2
0.08	$127,000	$54,800	2.3
0.25	$142,500	$59,739	2.4
0.17	$169,100	$76,434	2.2

DALLAS MSA HOUSING VALUE, FAMILY INCOME, AND FORECLOSURES

	2008 FORECLOSURES AND PREFORECLOSURES	2007 HOUSING UNITS	NUMBER OF HOUSING UNITS TO FORECLOSURES AND PREFORECLOSURES
United States	1,009,485	127,895,430	127
Texas	36,151	9,433,119	261
Counties			
Collin	1,510	276,951	183
Dallas	6,195	938,091	151
Delta	2		
Denton	396	218,775	552
Ellis	190	50,224	264
Hunt	49	34,585	706
Johnson	124	52,648	425
Kaufman	104	31,583	304
Parker	62	38,211	616
Rockwall	253	25,118	99
Tarrant	4,101	674,312	164
Wise	37		

NOTE:
County foreclosure data from foreclosure.com on 10/27/2008.
State foreclosure data from foreclosure.com on 10/16/2008.
Income and housing data from census.gov 2007 American Community Survey.
No data were available for blank cells.

% OF HOUSING UNITS UNDER FORECLOSURE OR PREFORECLOSURE	2007 MEDIAN VALUE OF OWNER-OCCUPIED HOUSING	2007 MEDIAN FAMILY INCOME	RATIO OF HOUSING VALUE TO MEDIAN FAMILY INCOME
0.79	$185,200	$58,526	3.2
0.38	$114,000	$52,355	2.2
0.55	$196,800	$92,351	2.1
0.66	$129,800	$51,780	2.5
0.18	$179,100	$87,084	2.1
0.38	$127,700	$63,676	2.0
0.14	$87,300	$52,017	1.7
0.24	$114,500	$56,734	2.0
0.33	$131,200	$59,623	2.2
0.16	$139,200	$67,808	2.1
1.01	$187,300	$86,689	2.2
0.61	$133,000	$62,490	2.1

DENVER MSA HOUSING VALUE, FAMILY INCOME, AND FORECLOSURES

	2008 FORECLOSURES AND PREFORECLOSURES	2007 HOUSING UNITS	NUMBER OF HOUSING UNITS TO FORECLOSURES AND PREFORECLOSURES
United States	1,009,485	127,895,430	127
Colorado	29,299	2,127,358	73
Counties			
Adams	4,885	162,097	33
Arapahoe	4,582	228,500	50
Broomfield	264		
Clear Creak	59		
Denver	6,120	274,253	45
Douglas	1,773	99,301	56
Elbert	156		
Gilpin	43		
Jefferson	3223	228,031	71
Park	141		

NOTE:
County foreclosure data from foreclosure.com on 11/10/2008.
State foreclosure data from foreclosure.com on 10/16/2008.
Income and housing data from census.gov 2007 American Community Survey.
No data were available for blank cells.

DETROIT MSA HOUSING VALUE, FAMILY INCOME, AND FORECLOSURES

	2008 FORECLOSURES AND PREFORECLOSURES	2007 HOUSING UNITS	NUMBER OF HOUSING UNITS TO FORECLOSURES AND PREFORECLOSURES
United States	1,009,485	127,895,430	127
Michigan	17,839	4,526,914	254
Counties			
Lapeer	137	35,786	261
Livingston	226	72,458	321
Macomb	1,596	352,987	221
Oakland	2,215	524,762	237
St. Clair	267	73,260	274
Wayne	6,522	839,201	129

NOTE:
County foreclosure data from foreclosure.com on 10/27/2008.
State foreclosure data from foreclosure.com on 10/20/2008.
Income and housing data from census.gov 2007 American Community Survey.

% OF HOUSING UNITS UNDER FORECLOSURE OR PREFORECLOSURE	2007 MEDIAN VALUE OF OWNER-OCCUPIED HOUSING	2007 MEDIAN FAMILY INCOME	RATIO OF HOUSING VALUE TO MEDIAN FAMILY INCOME
0.79	$185,200	$58,526	3.2
1.38	$232,900	$64,614	3.6
3.01	$199,900	$61,791	3.2
2.01	$235,500	$71,921	3.3
2.23	$234,500	$54,798	4.3
1.79	$337,700	$99,981	3.4
1.41	$255,200	$77,868	3.3

% OF HOUSING UNITS UNDER FORECLOSURE OR PREFORECLOSURE	2007 MEDIAN VALUE OF OWNER-OCCUPIED HOUSING	2007 MEDIAN FAMILY INCOME	RATIO OF HOUSING VALUE TO MEDIAN FAMILY INCOME
0.79	$185,200	$58,526	3.2
0.39	$153,300	$57,996	2.6
0.38	$165,100	$62,190	2.7
0.31	$232,800	$82,783	2.8
0.45	$171,900	$67,798	2.5
0.42	$222,700	$83,207	2.7
0.36	$154,800	$57,330	2.7
0.78	$137,300	$52,894	2.6

HOUSTON MSA HOUSING VALUE, FAMILY INCOME, AND FORECLOSURES

	2008 FORECLOSURES AND PREFORECLOSURES	2007 HOUSING UNITS	NUMBER OF HOUSING UNITS TO FORECLOSURES AND PREFORECLOSURES
United States	1,009,485	127,895,430	127
Texas	36,151	9,433,119	261
Counties			
Austin	9		
Brazoria	175	112,747	644
Chambers	0		
Fort Bend	904	148,756	165
Galveston	1,150	131,147	114
Harris	7,865	1,544,601	196
Liberty	31	28,295	913
Montgomery	785	156,042	199
San Jacinto	7		
Waller	21		

NOTE:
County foreclosure data from foreclosure.com on 11/1/2008.
State foreclosure data from foreclosure.com on 10/16/2008.
Income and housing data from census.gov 2007 American Community Survey.
No data were available for blank cells.

% OF HOUSING UNITS UNDER FORECLOSURE OR PREFORECLOSURE	2007 MEDIAN VALUE OF OWNER-OCCUPIED HOUSING	2007 MEDIAN FAMILY INCOME	RATIO OF HOUSING VALUE TO MEDIAN FAMILY INCOME
0.79	$185,200	$58,526	3.2
0.38	$114,000	$52,355	2.2
0.16	$136,700	$72,284	1.9
0.61	$168,800	$85,458	2.0
0.88	$136,300	$66,095	2.1
0.51	$131,700	$56,961	2.3
0.11	$84,500	$51,259	1.6
0.50	$150,400	$76,188	2.0

INDIANAPOLIS MSA HOUSING VALUE, FAMILY INCOME, AND FORECLOSURES

	2008 FORECLOSURES AND PREFORECLOSURES	2007 HOUSING UNITS	NUMBER OF HOUSING UNITS TO FORECLOSURES AND PREFORECLOSURES
United States	1,009,485	127,895,430	127
Indiana	6,587	2,777,953	422
Counties			
Boone	48		
Brown	7		
Hamilton	188	99,413	529
Hancock	74	27,480	371
Hendricks	100	54,708	547
Johnson	154	55,468	360
Marion	1,571	418,061	266
Morgan	82	28,688	350
Putnam	34		
Shelby	75		

NOTE:
County foreclosure data from foreclosure.com on 10/27/2008.
State foreclosure data from foreclosure.com on 10/20/2008.
Income and housing data from census.gov 2007 American Community Survey.
No data were available for blank cells.

% OF HOUSING UNITS UNDER FORECLOSURE OR PREFORECLOSURE	2007 MEDIAN VALUE OF OWNER-OCCUPIED HOUSING	2007 MEDIAN FAMILY INCOME	RATIO OF HOUSING VALUE TO MEDIAN FAMILY INCOME
0.79	$185,200	$58,526	3.2
0.24	$120,700	$55,781	2.2
0.19	$206,700	$93,597	2.2
0.27	$157,400	$71,170	2.2
0.18	$159,700	$73,499	2.2
0.28	$141,600	$74,359	1.9
0.38	$122,500	$55,386	2.2
0.29	$144,800	$59,383	2.4

ANSAS CITY MSA HOUSING VALUE, FAMILY INCOME, AND FORECLOSURES

	2008 FORECLOSURES AND PREFORECLOSURES	2007 HOUSING UNITS	NUMBER OF HOUSING UNITS TO FORECLOSURES AND PREFORECLOSURES
United States	1,009,485	127,895,430	127
Missouri	12,762	2,647,379	207
Counties			
Bates	8		
Caldwell	2		
Cass	354	38,828	110
Clay	754	84,850	113
Clinton	16		
Franklin, Kans.	14		
Jackson	3,613	316,315	88
Johnson	37		
Lafayette	27		
Leavenworth, Kans.	39	27,607	708
Linn, Kans.	7		
Miami, Kans.	18		
Platte	153	36,632	239
Ray	23		
Wyandotte, Kans.	268	67,600	252

NOTE:
County foreclosure data from foreclosure.com on 11/1/2008.
State foreclosure data from foreclosure.com on 10/20/2008.
Income and housing data from census.gov 2007 American Community Survey.
No data were available for blank cells.

LAS VEGAS MSA HOUSING VALUE, FAMILY INCOME, AND FORECLOSURES

	2008 FORECLOSURES AND PREFORECLOSURES	2007 HOUSING UNITS	NUMBER OF HOUSING UNITS TO FORECLOSURES AND PREFORECLOSURES
United States	1,009,485	127,895,430	127
Nevada	45,147	1,102,409	24
Counties			
Clark	39,891	788,080	20

NOTE:
County foreclosure data from foreclosure.com on 10/25/2008.
State foreclosure data from foreclosure.com on 10/16/2008.
Income and housing data from census.gov 2007 American Community Survey.

% OF HOUSING UNITS UNDER FORECLOSURE OR PREFORECLOSURE	2007 MEDIAN VALUE OF OWNER-OCCUPIED HOUSING	2007 MEDIAN FAMILY INCOME	RATIO OF HOUSING VALUE TO MEDIAN FAMILY INCOME
0.79	$185,200	$58,526	3.2
0.48	$131,900	$53,026	2.5
0.91	$153,600	$68,856	2.2
0.89	$155,600	$68,666	2.3
1.14	$134,300	$56,667	2.4
0.14	$171,000	$69,180	2.5
0.42	$190,900	$78,844	2.4
0.40	$98,600	$45,734	2.2

% OF HOUSING UNITS UNDER FORECLOSURE OR PREFORECLOSURE	2007 MEDIAN VALUE OF OWNER-OCCUPIED HOUSING	2007 MEDIAN FAMILY INCOME	RATIO OF HOUSING VALUE TO MEDIAN FAMILY INCOME
0.79	$185,200	$58,526	3.2
4.10	$315,200	$61,466	5.1
5.06	$315,300	$62,369	5.1

LOS ANGELES MSA HOUSING VALUE, FAMILY INCOME, AND FORECLOSURES

	2008 FORECLOSURES AND PREFORECLOSURES	2007 HOUSING UNITS	NUMBER OF HOUSING UNITS TO FORECLOSURES AND PREFORECLOS URES
United States	1,009,485	127,895,430	127
California	342,445	13,308,705	39
Counties			
Los Angeles	46,971	3,356,711	71
Orange	12,503	1,023,194	82
Ventura	4,222	269,879	64
Riverside	32,475	729,148	22
San Bernadino	26,973	667,836	25

NOTE:
County foreclosure data from foreclosure.com on 1/16/2009.
State foreclosure data from foreclosure.com on 10/20/2008.
Income and housing data from census.gov 2007 American Community Survey.

MIAMI MSA HOUSING VALUE, FAMILY INCOME, AND FORECLOSURES

	2008 FORECLOSURES AND PREFORECLOSURES	2007 HOUSING UNITS	NUMBER OF HOUSING UNITS TO FORECLOSURES AND PREFORECLOSURES
United States	1,009,485	127,895,430	127
Florida	173,231	8,716,601	50
Counties			
Broward	31,540	803,097	25
Miami-Dade	11,095	971,608	88
Palm Beach	18,122	638,609	35

NOTE:
County foreclosure data from foreclosure.com on 10/27/2008.
State foreclosure data from foreclosure.com on 10/16/2008.
Income and housing data from census.gov 2007 American Community Survey.

% OF HOUSING UNITS UNDER FORECLOSURE OR PREFORECLOSURE	2007 MEDIAN VALUE OF OWNER-OCCUPIED HOUSING	2007 MEDIAN FAMILY INCOME	RATIO OF HOUSING VALUE TO MEDIAN FAMILY INCOME
0.79	$185,200	$58,526	3.2
2.57	$535,700	$64,563	8.3
1.40	$550,000	$58,647	9.4
1.22	$656,600	$81,260	8.1
1.56	$631,000	$81,187	7.8
4.45	$395,100	$62,430	6.3
4.04	$363,700	$59,606	6.1

% OF HOUSING UNITS UNDER FORECLOSURE OR PREFORECLOSURE	2007 MEDIAN VALUE OF OWNER-OCCUPIED HOUSING	2007 MEDIAN FAMILY INCOME	RATIO OF HOUSING VALUE TO MEDIAN FAMILY INCOME
0.79	$185,200	$58,526	3.2
1.99	$230,600	$54,445	4.2
3.93	$302,500	$64,344	4.7
1.14	$318,100	$49,894	6.4
2.84	$308,900	$64,297	4.8

MILWAUKEE MSA HOUSING VALUE, FAMILY INCOME, AND FORECLOSURES

	2008 FORECLOSURES AND PREFORECLOSURES	2007 HOUSING UNITS	NUMBER OF HOUSING UNITS TO FORECLOSURES AND PREFORECLOSURES
United States	1,009,485	127,895,430	127
Wisconsin	9,499	2,558,278	269
Counties			
Milwaukee	6,193	410,771	66
Ozaukee	17	35,633	2,096
Washington	34	53,312	1,568
Waukesha	76	155,861	2,051

NOTE:
County foreclosure data from foreclosure.com on 10/27/2008.
State foreclosure data from foreclosure.com on 10/16/2008.
Income and housing data from census.gov 2007 American Community Survey.

MINNEAPOLIS/ST. PAUL MSA HOUSING VALUE, FAMILY INCOME, AND FORECLOSURES

	2008 FORECLOSURES AND PREFORECLOSURES	2007 HOUSING UNITS	NUMBER OF HOUSING UNITS TO FORECLOSURES AND PREFORECLOSURES
United States	1,009,485	127,895,430	127
Minnesota	8,834	2,304,473	261
Counties			
Anoka	443	124,577	281
Carver	287	33,353	116
Chisago	97		
Dakota	1,784	155,007	87
Hennepin	1,649	499,628	303
Isanti	94		
Pierce, Wisc.	36		
Ramsey	1,788	214,296	120
Scott	177	45,205	255
Sherburn	261	31,652	121
St Croix, Wisc.	118	33,145	281
Washington	241	88,606	368
Wright	707	47,915	68

NOTE:
County foreclosure data from foreclosure.com on 11/1/2008.
State foreclosure data from foreclosure.com on 10/20/2008.
Income and housing data from census.gov 2007 American Community Survey.
No data were available for blank cells.

% OF HOUSING UNITS UNDER FORECLOSURE OR PREFORECLOSURE	2007 MEDIAN VALUE OF OWNER-OCCUPIED HOUSING	2007 MEDIAN FAMILY INCOME	RATIO OF HOUSING VALUE TO MEDIAN FAMILY INCOME
0.79	$185,200	$58,526	3.2
0.37	$163,500	$60,634	2.7
1.51	$168,400	$53,123	3.2
0.05	$246,200	$90,015	2.7
0.06	$228,600	$75,816	3.0
0.05	$260,600	$86,244	3.0

% OF HOUSING UNITS UNDER FORECLOSURE OR PREFORECLOSURE	2007 MEDIAN VALUE OF OWNER-OCCUPIED HOUSING	2007 MEDIAN FAMILY INCOME	RATIO OF HOUSING VALUE TO MEDIAN FAMILY INCOME
0.79	$185,200	$58,526	3.2
0.38	$208,200	$66,809	3.1
0.36	$232,700	$74,304	3.1
0.86	$292,300	$96,885	3.0
1.15	$250,700	$88,115	2.8
0.33	$254,200	$80,804	3.1
0.83	$229,600	$69,407	3.3
0.39	$280,600	$87,633	3.2
0.82	$240,400	$76,902	3.1
0.36	$229,000	$75,264	3.0
0.27	$282,500	$90,520	3.1
1.48	$230,600	$72,792	3.2

NEW YORK MSA HOUSING VALUE, FAMILY INCOME, AND FORECLOSURES

	2008 FORECLOSURES AND PREFORECLOSURES	2007 HOUSING UNITS	NUMBER OF HOUSING UNITS TO FORECLOSURES AND PREFORECLOSURES
United States	1,009,485	127,895,430	127
New York	13,198	7,940,072	602
Counties			
Bergen, N.J.	867	349,534	403
Bronx	1,413	508,570	360
Essex, N.J.	1,778	311,180	175
Hudson, N.J.	759	254,780	336
Hunterdon, N.J.	107	48,753	456
Kings	3,653	959,465	263
Middlesex, N.J.	1,018	287,541	282
Monmouth, N.J.	994	255,256	257
Morris, N.J.	500	184,637	369
Nassau	236	458,577	1,943
New York	317	844,349	2,664
Ocean, N.J.	3,097	273,054	88
Passaic, N.J.	2,617	171,935	66
Pike, Pa.	71		
Putnam	35	36,470	1,042
Queens	4259	835,538	196
Richmond	1363	177,980	131
Rockland	32	98,599	3,081
Somerset, N.J.	328	121,430	370
Suffolk	221	544,470	2,464
Sussex, N.J.	323	60,581	188
Union, N.J.	1209	196,958	163
Westchester	202	358,372	1,774

NOTE:
County foreclosure data from foreclosure.com on 11/3/2008.
State foreclosure data from foreclosure.com on 10/20/2008.
Income and housing data from census.gov 2007 American Community Survey.
No data were available for blank cells.

% OF HOUSING UNITS UNDER FORECLOSURE OR PREFORECLOSURE	2007 MEDIAN VALUE OF OWNER-OCCUPIED HOUSING	2007 MEDIAN FAMILY INCOME	RATIO OF HOUSING VALUE TO MEDIAN FAMILY INCOME
0.79	$185,200	$58,526	3.2
0.17	$303,400	$62,138	4.9
0.25	$492,200	$98,618	5.0
0.28	$392,100	$37,977	10.3
0.57	$422,800	$65,806	6.4
0.30	$419,400	$53,528	7.8
0.22	$472,800	$117,001	4.0
0.38	$589,300	$47,761	12.3
0.35	$370,700	$87,929	4.2
0.39	$445,000	$94,301	4.7
0.27	$504,500	$111,464	4.5
0.05	$508,000	$104,430	4.9
0.04	$808,200	$69,202	11.7
1.13	$310,100	$71,149	4.4
1.52	$398,800	$67,345	5.9
0.10	$441,800	$91,434	4.8
0.51	$506,900	$60,085	8.4
0.77	$472,300	$78,571	6.0
0.03	$503,100	$94,910	5.3
0.27	$469,600	$111,809	4.2
0.04	$447,800	$95,373	4.7
0.53	$341,300	$88,989	3.8
0.61	$422,700	$76,220	5.5
0.06	$582,300	$99,243	5.9

ORLANDO MSA HOUSING VALUE, FAMILY INCOME, AND FORECLOSURES

	2008 FORECLOSURES AND PREFORECLOSURES	2007 HOUSING UNITS	NUMBER OF HOUSING UNITS TO FORECLOSURES AND PREFORECLOSURES
United States	1,009,485	127,895,430	127
Florida	173,231	8,716,601	50
Counties			
Lake	2,891	139,633	48
Orange	11,627	453,328	39
Osceola	4,789	117,637	25
Seminole	2,847	172,494	61

NOTE:
County foreclosure data from foreclosure.com on 11/1/2008.
State foreclosure data from foreclosure.com on 10/16/2008.
Income and housing data from census.gov 2007 American Community Survey.

PHILADELPHIA MSA HOUSING VALUE, FAMILY INCOME, AND FORECLOSURES

	2008 FORECLOSURES AND PREFORECLOSURES	2007 HOUSING UNITS	NUMBER OF HOUSING UNITS TO FORECLOSURES AND PREFORECLOSURES
United States	1,009,485	127,895,430	127
Pennsylvania	10,320	5,478,158	531
Counties			
Bucks	699	240,349	344
Burlington, N.J.	795	174,782	220
Camden, N.J.	1,219	205,341	168
Cecil, Md.	32	40,072	1,252
Chester	51	183,693	3,602
Delaware	133	220,842	1,660
Gloucester, N.J.	500	106,689	213
Montgomery	684	313,701	459
New Castle, Del.	150	212,143	1,414
Philadelphia	3,510	660,646	188
Salem	142	27,531	194

NOTE:
County foreclosure data from foreclosure.com on 11/10/2008.
State foreclosure data from foreclosure.com on 10/16/2008.
Income and housing data from census.gov 2007 American Community Survey.

% OF HOUSING UNITS UNDER FORECLOSURE OR PREFORECLOSURE	2007 MEDIAN VALUE OF OWNER-OCCUPIED HOUSING	2007 MEDIAN FAMILY INCOME	RATIO OF HOUSING VALUE TO MEDIAN FAMILY INCOME
0.79	$185,200	$58,526	3.2
1.99	$230,600	$54,445	4.2
2.07	$202,800	$54,181	3.7
2.56	$263,000	$57,167	4.6
4.07	$235,300	$51,772	4.5
1.65	$268,700	$68,492	3.9

% OF HOUSING UNITS UNDER FORECLOSURE OR PREFORECLOSURE	2007 MEDIAN VALUE OF OWNER-OCCUPIED HOUSING	2007 MEDIAN FAMILY INCOME	RATIO OF HOUSING VALUE TO MEDIAN FAMILY INCOME
0.79	$185,200	$58,526	3.2
0.19	$145,200	$58,148	2.5
0.29	$326,800	$85,568	3.8
0.45	$276,600	$87,270	3.2
0.59	$223,400	$70,087	3.2
0.08	$244,500	$73,998	3.3
0.03	$343,300	$101,896	3.4
0.06	$231,200	$74,696	3.1
0.47	$235,300	$81,944	2.9
0.22	$301,000	$88,178	3.4
0.07	$252,200	$76,153	3.3
0.53	$136,400	$44,855	3.0
0.52	$188,800	$69,414	2.7

PHOENIX MSA HOUSING VALUE, FAMILY INCOME, AND FORECLOSURES

	2008 FORECLOSURES AND PREFORECLOSURES	2007 HOUSING UNITS	NUMBER OF HOUSING UNITS TO FORECLOSURES AND PREFORECLOSURES
United States	1,009,485	127,895,430	127
Arizona	60,292	2,667,550	44
Counties			
Maricopa	49,751	1,528,852	31
Pinal	5,212	137,370	26

NOTE:
County foreclosure data from foreclosure.com on 10/27/2008.
State foreclosure data from foreclosure.com on 10/16/2008.
Income and housing data from census.gov 2007 American Community Survey.

PITTSBURGH MSA HOUSING VALUE, FAMILY INCOME, AND FORECLOSURES

	2008 FORECLOSURES AND PREFORECLOSURES	2007 HOUSING UNITS	NUMBER OF HOUSING UNITS TO FORECLOSURES AND PREFORECLOSURES
United States	1,009,485	127,895,430	127
Pennsylvania	10,320	5,478,158	531
Counties			
Allegheny	3,156	591,653	187
Armstrong	31	32,692	1,055
Beaver	94	79,476	845
Butler	78	77,012	987
Fayette	39	67,084	1,720
Washington	114	92,072	808
Westmoreland	175	166,088	949

NOTE:
County foreclosure data from foreclosure.com on 11/2/2008.
State foreclosure data from foreclosure.com on 10/16/2008.
Income and housing data from census.gov 2007 American Community Survey.

% OF HOUSING UNITS UNDER FORECLOSURE OR PREFORECLOSURE	2007 MEDIAN VALUE OF OWNER-OCCUPIED HOUSING	2007 MEDIAN FAMILY INCOME	RATIO OF HOUSING VALUE TO MEDIAN FAMILY INCOME
0.79	$185,200	$58,526	3.2
2.26	$236,500	$55,709	4.2
3.25	$268,900	$54,730	4.9
3.79	$197,500	$54,890	3.6

% OF HOUSING UNITS UNDER FORECLOSURE OR PREFORECLOSURE	2007 MEDIAN VALUE OF OWNER-OCCUPIED HOUSING	2007 MEDIAN FAMILY INCOME	RATIO OF HOUSING VALUE TO MEDIAN FAMILY INCOME
0.79	$185,200	$58,526	3.2
0.19	$145,200	$58,148	2.5
0.53	$113,800	$63,144	1.8
0.09	$90,800	$47,810	1.9
0.12	$113,500	$53,468	2.1
0.10	$149,400	$63,728	2.3
0.06	$84,700	$41,204	2.1
0.12	$128,000	$61,827	2.1
0.11	$123,100	$59,375	2.1

PORTLAND, ORE., MSA HOUSING VALUE, FAMILY INCOME, AND FORECLOSURES

	2008 FORECLOSURES AND PREFORECLOSURES	2007 HOUSING UNITS	NUMBER OF HOUSING UNITS TO FORECLOSURES AND PREFORECLOSURES
United States	1,009,485	127,895,430	127
Oregon	10,944	1,609,764	147
Counties			
Clackamas	1,284	151,828	118
Clark, Wash.	1,789	158,703	89
Columbia	155		
Multnomah	2,088	310,396	149
Skamania, Wash.	4		
Washington	1,310	205,363	157
Yamhill	253	35,561	141

NOTE:
County foreclosure data from foreclosure.com on 11/3/2008.
State foreclosure data from foreclosure.com on 10/20/2008.
Income and housing data from census.gov 2007 American Community Survey.
No data were available for blank cells.

SACRAMENTO MSA HOUSING VALUE, FAMILY INCOME, AND FORECLOSURES

	2008 FORECLOSURES AND PREFORECLOSURES	2007 HOUSING UNITS	NUMBER OF HOUSING UNITS TO FORECLOSURES AND PREFORECLOSURES
United States	1,009,485	127,895,430	127
California	342,445	13,308,705	39
Counties			
El Dorado	1,389	82,649	60
Placer	3,012	145,094	48
Sacramento	19,297	548,001	28
Yolo	1,317	71,794	55

NOTE:
County foreclosure data from foreclosure.com on 11/9/2008.
State foreclosure data from foreclosure.com on 10/20/2008.
Income and housing data from census.gov 2007 American Community Survey.

% OF HOUSING UNITS UNDER FORECLOSURE OR PREFORECLOSURE	2007 MEDIAN VALUE OF OWNER-OCCUPIED HOUSING	2007 MEDIAN FAMILY INCOME	RATIO OF HOUSING VALUE TO MEDIAN FAMILY INCOME
0.79	$185,200	$58,526	3.2
0.68	$236,600	$55,923	4.2
0.85	$350,300	$70,764	5.0
1.13	$277,400	$66,451	4.2
0.67	$285,900	$61,952	4.6
0.64	$326,000	$75,894	4.3
0.71	$237,000	$58,052	4.1

% OF HOUSING UNITS UNDER FORECLOSURE OR PREFORECLOSURE	2007 MEDIAN VALUE OF OWNER-OCCUPIED HOUSING	2007 MEDIAN FAMILY INCOME	RATIO OF HOUSING VALUE TO MEDIAN FAMILY INCOME
0.79	$185,200	$58,526	3.2
2.57	$535,700	$64,563	8.3
1.68	$506,500	$79,116	6.4
2.08	$483,700	$82,641	5.9
3.52	$370,600	$64,520	5.7
1.83	$444,100	$74,220	6.0

SAN ANTONIO MSA HOUSING VALUE, FAMILY INCOME, AND FORECLOSURES

	2008 FORECLOSURES AND PREFORECLOSURES	2007 HOUSING UNITS	NUMBER OF HOUSING UNITS TO FORECLOSURES AND PREFORECLOSURES
United States	1,009,485	127,895,430	127
Texas	36,151	9,433,119	261
Counties			
Atascosa	8		
Bandera	4		
Bexar	2,240	603,576	269
Comal	156	44,578	286
Guadalupe	116	41,486	358
Kendall	17		
Medina	17		
Wilson	13		

NOTE:
County foreclosure data from foreclosure.com on 11/1/2008.
State foreclosure data from foreclosure.com on 10/16/2008.
Income and housing data from census.gov 2007 American Community Survey.
No data were available for blank cells.

SAN DIEGO MSA HOUSING VALUE, FAMILY INCOME, AND FORECLOSURES

	2008 FORECLOSURES AND PREFORECLOSURES	2007 HOUSING UNITS	NUMBER OF HOUSING UNITS TO FORECLOSURES AND PREFORECLOSURES
United States	1,009,485	127,895,430	127
California	342,445	13,308,705	39
Counties			
San Diego	23,996	1,133,069	47

NOTE:
County foreclosure data from foreclosure.com on 10/27/2008.
State foreclosure data from foreclosure.com on 10/20/2008.
Income and housing data from census.gov 2007 American Community Survey.

% OF HOUSING UNITS UNDER FORECLOSURE OR PREFORECLOSURE	2007 MEDIAN VALUE OF OWNER-OCCUPIED HOUSING	2007 MEDIAN FAMILY INCOME	RATIO OF HOUSING VALUE TO MEDIAN FAMILY INCOME
0.79	$185,200	$58,526	3.2
0.38	$114,000	$52,355	2.2
0.37	$113,200	$52,558	2.2
0.35	$165,600	$65,455	2.5
0.28	$142,300	$65,250	2.2

% OF HOUSING UNITS UNDER FORECLOSURE OR PREFORECLOSURE	2007 MEDIAN VALUE OF OWNER-OCCUPIED HOUSING	2007 MEDIAN FAMILY INCOME	RATIO OF HOUSING VALUE TO MEDIAN FAMILY INCOME
0.79	$185,200	$58,526	3.2
2.57	$535,700	$64,563	8.3
2.12	$556,500	$61,794	9.0

SAN FRANCISCO MSA HOUSING VALUE, FAMILY INCOME, AND FORECLOSURES

	2008 FORECLOSURES AND PREFORECLOSURES	2007 HOUSING UNITS	NUMBER OF HOUSING UNITS TO FORECLOSURES AND PREFORECLOSURES
United States	1,009,485	127,895,430	127
California	342,445	13,308,705	39
Counties			
Alameda	10,108	560,311	55
Contra Costa	13,087	388,376	30
Marin	638	107,927	169
Napa	802	52,694	66
San Francisco	842	356,462	423
San Mateo	1,968	266,469	135
Santa Clara	7,393	609,928	83
Solano	5,475	148,456	27
Sonoma	2,962	195,525	66

NOTE:
County foreclosure data from foreclosure.com on 1/16/2009.
State foreclosure data from foreclosure.com on 10/20/2008.
Income and housing data from census.gov 2007 American Community Survey.

SEATTLE MSA HOUSING VALUE, FAMILY INCOME, AND FORECLOSURES

	2008 FORECLOSURES AND PREFORECLOSURES	2007 HOUSING UNITS	NUMBER OF HOUSING UNITS TO FORECLOSURES AND PREFORECLOSURES
United States	1,009,485	127,895,430	127
Washington	15,064	2,744,324	182
Counties			
King	3,275	816,845	249
Pierce	3,095	314,545	102
Snohomish	1,733	275,822	159

NOTE:
County foreclosure data from foreclosure.com on 11/1/2008.
State foreclosure data from foreclosure.com on 10/20/2008.
Income and housing data from census.gov 2007 American Community Survey.

% OF HOUSING UNITS UNDER FORECLOSURE OR PREFORECLOSURE	2007 MEDIAN VALUE OF OWNER-OCCUPIED HOUSING	2007 MEDIAN FAMILY INCOME	RATIO OF HOUSING VALUE TO MEDIAN FAMILY INCOME
0.79	$185,200	$58,526	3.2
2.57	$535,700	$64,563	8.3
1.80	$633,000	$81,341	7.8
3.37	$618,800	$87,435	7.1
0.59	$895,100	$104,750	8.5
1.52	$638,600	$77,480	8.2
0.24	$789,400	$81,136	9.7
0.74	$807,400	$94,517	8.5
1.21	$725,800	$96,884	7.5
3.69	$427,500	$74,628	5.7
1.51	$611,300	$75,319	8.1

% OF HOUSING UNITS UNDER FORECLOSURE OR PREFORECLOSURE	2007 MEDIAN VALUE OF OWNER-OCCUPIED HOUSING	2007 MEDIAN FAMILY INCOME	RATIO OF HOUSING VALUE TO MEDIAN FAMILY INCOME
0.79	$185,200	$58,526	3.2
0.55	$267,600	$63,705	4.2
0.40	$433,300	$85,828	5.0
0.98	$285,100	$66,019	4.3
0.63	$346,100	$74,952	4.6

ST. LOUIS MSA HOUSING VALUE, FAMILY INCOME, AND FORECLOSURES

	2008 FORECLOSURES AND PREFORECLOSURES	2007 HOUSING UNITS	NUMBER OF HOUSING UNITS TO FORECLOSURES AND PREFORECLOSURES
United States	1,009,485	127,895,430	127
Missouri	12,762	2,647,379	207
Counties			
Bond, Ill.	7		
Calhoun, Ill.	2		
Clinton, Ill.	7		
Franklin	194	42,981	222
Jefferson	520	86,183	166
Jersey, Ill.	13		
Lincoln	46		
Macoupin, Ill.	28		
Madison, Ill.	1,420	117,227	83
Monroe, Ill.	12		
St. Charles	757	134,437	178
St. Clair, Ill.	1,963	114,541	58
St. Louis	3,257	435,236	134
St. Louis City	1,832	179,797	98
Warren	24		
Washington	20		

NOTE:
County foreclosure data from foreclosure.com on 11/10/2008.
State foreclosure data from foreclosure.com on 10/20/2008.
Income and housing data from census.gov 2007 American Community Survey.
No data were available for blank cells.

% OF HOUSING UNITS UNDER FORECLOSURE OR PREFORECLOSURE	2007 MEDIAN VALUE OF OWNER-OCCUPIED HOUSING	2007 MEDIAN FAMILY INCOME	RATIO OF HOUSING VALUE TO MEDIAN FAMILY INCOME
0.79	$185,200	$58,526	3.2
0.48	$131,900	$53,026	2.5
0.45	$143,700	$57,942	2.5
0.60	$152,500	$63,228	2.4
1.21	$123,800	$61,869	2.0
0.56	$195,700	$78,215	2.5
1.71	$122,500	$56,855	2.2
0.75	$182,000	$71,148	2.6
1.02	$128,300	$42,115	3.0

TAMPA/ST. PETERSBURG MSA HOUSING VALUE, FAMILY INCOME, AND FORECLOSURES

	2008 FORECLOSURES AND PREFORECLOSURES	2007 HOUSING UNITS	NUMBER OF HOUSING UNITS TO FORECLOSURES AND PREFORECLOSURES
United States	1,009,485	127,895,430	127
Florida	173,231	8,716,601	50
Counties			
Hernando	1,795	80,295	45
Hillsborough	11,314	515,881	46
Pasco	4,761	218,065	46
Pinellas	6,837	499,513	73

NOTE:
County foreclosure data from foreclosure.com on 11/1/2008.
State foreclosure data from foreclosure.com on 10/16/2008.
Income and housing data from census.gov 2007 American Community Survey.

% OF HOUSING UNITS UNDER FORECLOSURE OR PREFORECLOSURE	2007 MEDIAN VALUE OF OWNER-OCCUPIED HOUSING	2007 MEDIAN FAMILY INCOME	RATIO OF HOUSING VALUE TO MEDIAN FAMILY INCOME
0.79	$185,200	$58,526	3.2
1.99	$230,600	$54,445	4.2
2.24	$172,400	$52,234	3.3
2.19	$222,800	$61,570	3.6
2.18	$169,700	$54,145	3.1
1.37	$204,700	$57,403	3.6

VIRGINIA BEACH MSA HOUSING VALUE, FAMILY INCOME, AND FORECLOSURES

	2008 FORECLOSURES AND PREFORECLOSURES	2007 HOUSING UNITS	NUMBER OF HOUSING UNITS TO FORECLOSURES AND PREFORECLOSURES
United States	1,009,485	127,895,430	126.7
Virginia	7,380	3,273,206	443.5
Counties			
Chesapeake	145	82,084	566.1
Currituck, N.C.	27		
Gloucester	17		
Hampton	62	59,857	965.4
Isle of Wight	16		
James City	16		
Mathews	4		
Newport News	89	78,333	880.1
Norfolk	182	95,511	524.8
Poquoson	5		
Portsmouth	103	42,780	415.3
Suffolk	63	32,335	513.3
Surry	4		
Virginia Beach	214	174,669	816.2
Willamsburg	0		
York	9		

NOTE:
County foreclosure data from foreclosure.com on 11/5/2008.
State foreclosure data from foreclosure.com on 10/16/2008.
Income and housing data from census.gov 2007 American Community Survey.
No data were available for blank cells.

% OF HOUSING UNITS UNDER FORECLOSURE OR PREFORECLOSURE	2007 MEDIAN VALUE OF OWNER-OCCUPIED HOUSING	2007 MEDIAN FAMILY INCOME	RATIO OF HOUSING VALUE TO MEDIAN FAMILY INCOME
0.79	$185,200	$58,526	3.2
0.23	$244,200	$66,886	3.7
0.18	$267,000	$71,511	3.7
0.10	$188,600	$56,282	3.4
0.11	$190,700	$54,860	3.5
0.19	$200,100	$47,504	4.2
0.24	$179,300	$49,544	3.6
0.19	$250,200	$68,595	3.6
0.12	$282,400	$70,173	4.0

WASHINGTON, D.C., MSA HOUSING VALUE, FAMILY INCOME, AND FORECLOSURES

	2008 FORECLOSURES AND PREFORECLOSURES	2007 HOUSING UNITS	NUMBER OF HOUSING UNITS TO FORECLOSURES AND PREFORECLOSURES
United States	1,009,485	127,895,430	127
Counties			
Alexandria	92	70,265	764
Arlington	88	101,173	1,150
Calvert, Md.	53	32,372	611
Charles, Md.	132	52,630	399
Clarke	23		
Fairfax	1,431	392,338	274
Fairfax City	63		
Falls Church	13		
Fauquier	88	26,466	301
Frederick, Md.	208	86,154	414
Fredericksberg	39		
Loudoun	576	101,563	176
Manassas	240		
Manassas Park	0		
Montgomery, Md.	550	361,810	658
Prince Georges, Md.	1,182	319,915	271
Prince William	1,696	133,853	79
Spotsylvania	251	44,721	178
Stafford	240	42,598	177
Warren	84		
Washington, D.C.	338	284,235	841

NOTE:
County foreclosure data from foreclosure.com on 11/5/2008.
Income and housing data from census.gov 2007 American Community Survey.
No data were available for blank cells.

% OF HOUSING UNITS UNDER FORECLOSURE OR PREFORECLOSURE	2007 MEDIAN VALUE OF OWNER-OCCUPIED HOUSING	2007 MEDIAN FAMILY INCOME	RATIO OF HOUSING VALUE TO MEDIAN FAMILY INCOME
0.79	$185,200	$58,526	3.2
0.13	$555,100	$102,435	5.4
0.09	$596,600	$127,179	4.7
0.16	$425,600	$104,874	4.1
0.25	$371,100	$92,389	4.0
0.36	$568,900	$122,027	4.7
0.33	$445,600	$103,705	4.3
0.24	$378,500	$92,430	4.1
0.57	$544,400	$128,856	4.2
0.15	$524,700	$108,464	4.8
0.37	$354,600	$78,294	4.5
1.27	$435,100	$93,002	4.7
0.56	$349,100	$82,981	4.2
0.56	$411,100	$100,519	4.1
0.12	$450,900	$66,672	6.8

Insight and
Decision Guide

The trends described here shape everyday life. They describe some of the results of decisions about housing locations, transportation options, energy use, and local governments' taxing and spending. They capture realities that everyone must navigate, including the President of the United States; the chairman of the Federal Reserve Bank; the CEOs of JPMorgan Chase, Bank of America, Goldman Sachs, Fannie Mae, and Freddie Mac; home builders and developers large and small; state and local government officials; and citizens who are deciding where to live, work, study, shop, and play. Failure to identify and interpret these trends will cause each of these decision makers to sail blind.

Here are a few questions that decision makers can answer to guide their journeys through the next years:

Chapter 1
1. In which parts of metropolitan areas have foreclosures been most frequent? What are three possible explanations for these patterns?
2. Which roles played by financial and mortgage-lending manipulations, public policy goals, and political calculations created conditions in which the foreclosure and financial crises occurred?
3. If purchases of new large suburban homes are not reliable investments for profitable resales, what will be some consequences for cities and suburbs as the American dream shifts characteristics and direction?

Chapters 2 and 3
1. Why have per capita and family incomes been stabilizing or increasing in many cities more than in their suburbs?
2. Why have relative incomes of non-Hispanic whites risen in many cities while relative incomes of Hispanics and African-Americans have risen in many suburbs?
3. If old neighborhoods have been rising in relative incomes and this forecasts a stronger future for their cities, which suburbs will be vulnerable to deterioration?

Chapter 4
1. Can households change their location and transportation decisions and reduce average vehicle miles traveled?
2. Which obstacles impede expanding metropolitan transit capacity?
3. Can federal and state public policy incentives increase transit capacity, reduce average vehicle miles traveled, and reward behavior that reduces CO_2 emissions?

Chapters 5 and 6
1. Have states' smart growth policies coped with local government fragmentation, stimulated compact development, and reduced CO_2 emissions?
2. If households' location and transportation decisions are keys to combating climate change, how might public policies influence these decisions?

Index

About the Author

William H. Lucy is the Lawrence Lewis Jr. Professor of Urban and Environmental Planning at the University of Virginia. He is the author of *Close to Power: Setting Priorities with Elected Officials* and (with David L. Phillips) *Tomorrow's Cities, Tomorrow's Suburbs*, both published by APA Planners Press.